Michael Grose is one of Australia's most popular writers and speakers on parenting and family matters. The author of five books for parents, he has written in excess of 200 columns that have appeared in newspapers and magazines throughout Australia. He also gives over 80 presentations a year throughout Australia promoting healthy family relationships within schools, the workplace and the broader community. With humour and empathy Michael shows parents how to raise happy, confident kids and enjoy family life.

A former primary teacher, he has worked with children all his professional life. Young Leaders, his popular leadership program for young people, is conducted in schools in every state in Australia.

Michael is married with three children and lives on the Mornington Peninsula near Melbourne.

For more information and practical ideas to help you raise happy, resilient children and young people visit Michael's website: www.Parentingideas.com.au

Also by Michael Grose

A Man's Guide to Raising Kids
Working Parents
Great Ideas for (Tired) Parents
Raising Happy Kids
One Step Ahead: Raising 3–12 year olds

WHY FIRST-BORNS RULE THE WORLD AND LAST-BORNS WANT TO CHANGE IT

MICHAEL GROSE

RANDOM HOUSE AUSTRALIA

Random House Australia Pty Ltd
Level 3, 100 Pacific Highway, North Sydney, NSW 2060
http://www.randomhouse.com.au

Sydney New York Toronto
London Auckland Johannesburg

First published by Random House Australia 2003

National Library of Australia
  Cataloguing-in-Publication Entry

  Grose, Michael, 1955– .
  Why first-borns rule the world and last-borns want to change it.

  ISBN 978 1 74051 198 8.
  ISBN 1 74051 198 0.

  1. Birth-order. 2. Child psychology. 3. Parenting.
  I. Title.

  305.231

Cover photograph: Getty Images
Cover design by Greendot Design
Typeset in 11/14 pt Adobe Garamond by Midland Typesetters, Maryborough, Victoria
Printed and bound by Griffin Press, South Australia

Contents

Chapter 1

WHAT'S ALL THE FUSS ABOUT BIRTH ORDER?

The position in the family leaves an indelible stamp.
Alfred Adler

'I can't believe how different my two boys are, even though they were born only 18 months apart. It is as if they have two different fathers,' said a mother during a parenting seminar. I have heard hundreds of variations of this statement over the 14 years I have been involved in parenting education. The notion of the differences between children within a family has always fascinated me. The fact that a group of children can come from the same genetic pool, be brought up by the same parents, in the same neighbourhood, and go to the same schools and yet be so fundamentally diverse is one of the mysteries of human development. I figured that I have talked about the effects of birth order and thought about the effects of birth order for many years, so now it was time to put some answers down in a book.

A child's position in his or her family impacts on the child's personality, behaviour, learning and ultimately his or her earning power. Most people have an intuitive knowledge that birth order somehow has an impact on development but they underestimate how far-reaching and just how significant that impact really is. As we currently head down the track of genetic engineering, community concerns can be heard loud and clear about the possibility of cloning children. An understanding of the impact of birth order on a child's development should allay the fears of those who look toward a brave new world heralded by 'Dolly the sheep'. Genetic engineering may mean that while we are able to produce children with the same physical characteristics, they certainly wouldn't behave in the same ways, think the same or achieve at the same rate at school or later on at work. The birth position of these children, assuming that family size varies, would ensure that we would be able to tell these children apart. They may look the same but they would not act or behave in the same ways. Their family position would ensure that there would be sufficient differences to make life more than interesting.

The recognition of the effect of birth order on children and adults is only relatively recent. Austrian psychoanalyst Alfred Adler early last century introduced his theories on the way birth order affects personality and the notion has moved in and out of fashion ever since. In many ways it had been placed in the realms of 'pop' psychology (good fun to play with but was there any substance to it?) until researcher Frank Sulloway came along in the latter part of the century and added some much-needed scientific rigour to the concept. Sulloway's work, made public in his 1996 book *Born to Rebel*, has added legitimacy and substance to birth-order theory.

As a result of 26 years of exhaustive research Sulloway maintained that the single best predictor of either leadership or revolutionary creativity was birth order. After systematically studying the lives of 6000 North American and European scientists, he discovered that their place in their family coincided with their propensity to accept or challenge new ideas and to support the status quo. First-borns were the staunch defenders of conventional thinking while later-borns were the champions of innovation and discovery.

Sulloway's work also confirmed the existence of a set of personal characteristics and qualities shared by the different birth positions. In his metastudy of 196 birth-order studies, Sulloway confirmed the following propositions:

- first-borns are more conforming, traditional and more likely to identify with their parents
- first-borns are more achievement oriented, organised and responsible than later-borns
- later-borns are more gregarious, cooperative and easygoing
- first-borns are more jealous, neurotic, intense, upset by defeat and experience more stress
- first-borns are more assertive and extraverted than later-borns.

Does birth-order theory really work?

Birth-order theory works much of the time for most people but it is not foolproof. There are many influences on personality development, including genetics, temperament, family style and broad environmental and social factors. Birth order is just one factor that impacts on personality development but a powerful one nonetheless. There are exceptions to birth-order theory but they make sense when you look at the whole picture of a person and understand how birth order works and how variables impact on the rules.

According to Alfred Adler there are five positions that a child can be born into: – first-born, second, middle, only and youngest. Many theorists commonly reduce birth order to three positions: first-borns, second-borns and youngest children. I refer to these three positions plus I include a chapter on only or single children. Only children are in fact first-borns who have never been displaced. Kevin Leman in *The New Birth Order Book* refers to only children as 'super first-borns' as they share many of the characteristics of first-borns however they tend to be magnified in many of these children. Middle children and second-born children also share common traits and circumstances. These days with families becoming smaller many second children are in fact middle children. I have included a chapter on two- and three-children families, as first- and second-borns in these families can be different to those children in larger families.

In the past when families were bigger, and family planning was ad hoc and relatively ineffective, birth-order theory became a little blurred. For instance, I am the youngest in my family but there is a six-year gap between my next sibling and myself. In many ways I am like an eldest-born and I also share many characteristics of youngest and only children. Like youngest children I was never displaced and my parents were, to put it politely, tired by the time I came along. My eldest siblings had well and truly broken them in for me so I had a fairly easy ride. I also spent a great deal of time in the company of my parents rather than other siblings so I tended to be 'mature' for my age, which is both a curse and benefit that many only or single children share.

In this era of small, planned families birth-order theory is more relevant than ever. We are now witnessing the emergence of children with easily defined birth-order personalities. When families are small and the age gap between siblings is two years or less then competition for spaces in families is at its most fierce. These are ideal conditions for birth-order theory to come to life. Now more than ever birth-order theory adds a clearly defined, easily identifiable dimension to children's personality development.

Why birth-order theory works

Birth-order theory works so well because we are social beings trying to find a niche in our social groups. The first social group we belong to is our family. Within our family we compete with our siblings for different places, positions and niches. When one position, say the responsible child, is filled then we look for another. So younger children tend to define themselves according to whatever territory is left over once the eldest has staked his or her claim. When we understand that the prime motivation of any child is to find his or her special place or niche in the family then birth order begins to make sense. It is folly to try to understand a child's personality development or behaviour without taking into account the personalities and interests of others in the family. When you understand the rules of birth order and consider all the variables then an accurate picture begins to form of children's birth-order personality.

Birth-order theory is about understanding your place in your family and its impact on your life. Whether you are first or last, first of two children, an only child or a twin, or stuck in the middle of a large tribe, your position affects your life in many ways. It will influence your levels of achievement at school. It will help determine the job you choose and even how long you work. It will help determine the spouse you choose. Your birth order and your partner's birth position will impact on the success of your partnership. It will also impact on the choice and number of friends that you have. It will influence your health and wellbeing, even determining your likelihood of heart disease. Yes, first-borns are more prone to heart disorders than any other position, presumably as this group experience more stress and anxiety. But your birth order is a predictor not the sole determinant of your future success, health and wellbeing. As cognitive beings we can decide how we act, feel and behave at any stage in our lives. We are not at the whim of genetics or locked into behaving in predetermined ways. So birth order presents possibilities not certainties. But the possibilities and patterns are intriguing!

Answer this question to test your knowledge of birth order:

Which of the following descriptions best fits the (1) first-born, (2) middle-born, (3) youngest, and (4) only child?

(a) I don't know how he does it; his room is a mess but whenever he wants something he knows exactly where it is.

(b) That girl is a real manipulator. Charming as anything but she knows how to get her own way. She'll be a great salesperson one day.

(c) Phil is a budding scientist. He is fantastic at math, but he drives people crazy with his precision and dedication to perfection.

(d) Joan has heaps of friends. She is hard to sum up but she is terrific with people and a first-class negotiator. She'll end up a diplomat some day, working for her eldest brother who is bound to be prime minister.

(e) Col gets on better with older people than his peers. Many people think he is self-centred as he is not very good at sharing.

Answers: (a) 1; (b) 3; (c) 1; (d) 2; (e) 4

My guess is you know a great deal about birth order already and you probably matched most of your answers with mine. Either that or you are way off the mark and your notion of birth order will reflect your personal experiences. If you picked (a) as being a first-born then you know that first-borns may not always have things in order but they like to have things under control. Their room or desk may be messy but they know where everything is. It's a first-born trait. If you recognise yourself in (b) then chances are that you were the youngest in your family who became adept at putting more capable elder siblings in your service. You may have been a charmer but you knew exactly what you were doing. If you have an eye for detail, and accuracy in everything you do is important, then you may recognise yourself in Phil in (c). Middle kids are generally the most gregarious individuals and make great negotiators – like Joan in (b) they make great 'people' people. If you picked Col in (e) as an only or single child you may be aware that sometimes these children just don't have the same opportunities to share their time, space and possessions as other children.

Not every child will fit these characteristics. Sometimes first-borns seem more like youngest children and second-borns may seem more like first-borns. As you will discover seconds can function like first-borns – in fact, there can be more than one first-born in a family. But more about this later. There are many variables in birth-order theory but once you understand the basic concepts then it is easy to account for many of the differences. For instance, my office manager is the fourth of five children but she functions like a first-born. She is efficient, well-organised and pays attention to fine details. She is adept at making up systems and procedures that help the office run like clockwork. These are typical first-born traits so I was a little surprised to find that she was not the eldest. After a few conversations I soon learned that she was treated like a first-born in her family of origin. There was also a five-year gap between her and her elder sibling, which effectively gave her first-born status over any sibling who followed. She was given plenty of responsibilities around the house however there were few expectations for her younger brother to take on any responsibility at home. With a sibling to follow and a mother who worked full-time it fell on Sue to shoulder much of the parenting of the younger sibling. Cooking, bathing and baby-sitting were just some of the extra responsibilities that Sue took on. With this background it is little wonder that Sue is an organisational wizard. From a young age she learned how to juggle a number of different tasks, prioritising jobs and working systematically through a series of set tasks until each job was finished. She may have been born later in the family but she functions like a first-born who is used to being in charge and in control of most situations involving others.

How birth-order knowledge helps you

When you look at others through the lens of birth order you gain a keener understanding of the differences between people. You will also begin to develop techniques and ideas that will help you relate to others in your family and mix more successfully with your colleagues at work or in business. You will also learn more about yourself, as birth-order knowledge is self-knowledge.

Some years ago after conducting a seminar about birth order a participant nearly knocked me down in his excitement to tell me how the lights went on for him when he heard what I had to say. For years he and his elder brother had kept their distance, as each thought the other sibling should be more like him. He begged for a tape of the presentation so he could send it to his sibling and shed some light on their differences. Birth-order knowledge according to this fellow provided the key to understanding the differences between him and his brother.

Effective communicators are adept at appreciating and working with people who are fundamentally different to themselves. Like-minded people tend to mix together. Next time you are in a bar or other public place where people socialise notice how similar the people are to each other as they mix in their various groups. People within each group will more than likely dress in similar styles, be of a similar age and will probably even live in similar types of areas. We feel comfortable amongst people who look, act and think the same as we do. We identify with others who have the same outlook on life and also those who have the same birth position.

But we can become too comfortable for our own good. As many managers and small business people are aware they can be their own worst enemy when choosing their staff. Unless they are aware, there is a real tendency to choose like-minded souls rather than people who are different. If we value organisational skills then there is every chance we will hire someone who is highly organised. If we are highly creative and value spontaneity then there is every chance that we will select people of a similar ilk. Effective teams are made up of diverse characters who have not only different skills but also a variety of personal characteristics, qualities and working styles.

Birth-order knowledge will help you understand the personalities of others who are different to you. It may help you understand why that first-born picky boss is such a perfectionist, intolerant of even the smallest mistake. It may be that the receptionist who drives you crazy with her consistent friendliness just happens to be a middle child who gets on better with people than someone from any other birth-order position. It could well be that the person sharing the next desk who never worries about turning her computer off at the end of the day is a youngest and can't see the point in such an exercise. She probably never unpacked her bag as a child as her mother either did that for her or was too tired to bother insisting that she do so.

If you share an office with a person who takes every criticism personally, and wants to be in charge of everything from the photocopier to the weekly footy sweep, then take your hat off to a first-born. Understand that your bossy workmate was probably the eldest who was left in charge of younger siblings for long periods of time. Many first-borns just hate criticism but love to have a finger in every organisational pie. If it drives you crazy that your best friend always dresses in the latest fashion and never seems to have a hair out of place while you always look as if you are about to get dressed, then the chances are that your friend is an eldest child, while you are a later-born. Understanding and appreciating people who are different to us is a key to working and living successfully with others.

Birth-order knowledge is a useful tool to employ at work. Not long ago I was discussing business with a friend who was lamenting the fact that despite running an efficient operation his company's sales had been declining for a number of quarters. The firm sold educational and training solutions to medium to large businesses. I was surprised to hear about their falling sales as their product was first-rate, their trainers highly regarded in the industry and their marketing systems and procedures were excellent. My colleague didn't have specialised salespeople, however, he split the sales task between his administrative team. He had given them what appeared to be ample training in selling processes and telephone techniques but it appeared that their hearts just weren't in the job. I asked my colleague if he knew the birth-order position of the people who did most of the selling of his programs and resources. He shrugged his shoulders and gave me a blank look. I suggested that he take a birth-order audit of his workforce and also the telemarketers to whom he outsourced some of his selling. He agreed but he wasn't sure why I wanted the audit. I wasn't surprised with the results of his audit. The workforce of his small company was made up entirely of first-borns or functional first-borns. These people love organising but are not natural salespeople. My suggestion was to employ a later-born as he had the wrong people selling for him. Let the first-borns do what they do best – managing, organising, creating and maintaining systems – and let a natural-born salesperson – a youngest – do the selling. It was no wonder he thought that his administrative staff didn't have their hearts in the job of selling despite the incentive of hefty bonuses. He had the wrong people for the job. My colleague took my advice and was surprised how different the approach of youngest-borns was to the selling job. He commented later that they seemed to actually enjoy the whole selling process. It would be simplistic to think that all those born youngest would make great salespeople and that first-borns can't sell. But it is no co-incidence that more youngest-borns tend to be attracted to selling than those in any other birth position. It is no coincidence that law and accountancy contain more first-borns than any other birth position. The attention to detail required and the relatively solitary nature of these professions suits the birth-order personality of first-borns.

Many years ago I worked in a parenting education centre that used birth-order knowledge to great effect. In fact, my colleagues and I would use this knowledge to win over audiences and clients with whom we worked. My colleagues and I would conduct educative counselling sessions in front of audiences of up to 200 people. This approach was educative rather than therapeutic as we used a 'live' family to demonstrate many prin-ciples of effective parenting. Early in the sessions we would ask the parents to describe the personalities and behaviour of one of their children, usually the first-born. Even if we didn't ask them to start with the first-born most parents would begin with that child without any prompting. It seems that the eldest sets the tone for those who are to follow. Once we heard a description of that child we would then ask the parents to listen while we described the other children in their family. Most of the time our descriptions of other children were accurate enough to amaze both the parents in focus and the audience. There was no magic at all in this piece of theatrics, just the application of some solid psychological principles. Once we knew one child's personality and had knowledge of the family structure it was relatively easy to paint a picture of the behaviour, personalities and even interests of the other children. This little piece of magic gave my colleagues and me enormous credibility among the audience.

Birth-order knowledge helps you to better understand the nature of the relationship with your siblings. When people find out that I am interested in birth-order theory and practice they often give me their personal birth-order stories. Many of the personal accounts indicate dissatisfaction with the treatment that siblings received compared to them. First-borns had more to complain about than any other position, citing favouritism and preferred treatment being given to younger siblings.

Here is an example:

> I am the eldest in my family, with my sister being two and a half years younger than me. While my sister and I always got along famously as we were growing up (both now in our mid-20s) I always felt that there were certain expectations on me, especially from my father, that my sister was free from, and that she could get away with murder if she wanted to. I think one of the most annoying things for my sister was when she was always met with 'Oh, you're Lisa's sister.' So you can imagine her delight, since I have moved back to our home town after being away for several years, that I now get 'Oh, you're Erin's sister.' I, on the other hand, have always been greeted with 'Oh, you're Neil's daughter,' which automatically puts me in good behaviour mode, because 'this person knows Dad and I wouldn't want to embarrass him or let him down'. From my point of view, being the eldest child gave me the raw deal, even though my parents intended to treat us equally (Lisa Sullivan).

Birth-order knowledge helps you to better understand your children and yourself. Parents tend to define their children according to their children's positions. 'He is my eldest' or 'She is the baby of the family' are descriptors that many people are familiar with. It is less relevant how parents define their children than how children see themselves in relation to their siblings. First-born children tend to have a different set of characteristics than later-born children so parenting principles that may be successful with one child can have the opposite effect with another child. Youngest-born children can turn dependency into an art form, which can be disconcerting to parents who value and promote independence. 'How can I get this child to stand on her own two feet? is the lament of many parents about their youngest-borns. But these children survive and thrive as they become adept at getting others to solve their problems and difficulties. Children often use their position in their family to get their needs met. While youngest children may become expert at manipulating siblings, older children may push themselves to great lengths to get affirmation and approval from their parents.

Birth-order theory is also relevant for stepfamilies. In fact, I am astonished at how many parents forget to factor in the position of each child in their original families when the two families join. The producers of the *Brady Bunch* TV series of the 1970s, that presented a saccharine-sweet view of stepfamilies, obviously knew nothing of birth-order theory when they devised and scripted that show. The blending of three girls and three boys from different families but each with a stepsibling of a similar age is a recipe for stepsibling rivalry if ever there was one. If the writers wanted to stick to reality then the two eldest siblings, who were similar in age, should have been portrayed as being in constant battle to assert the rights of being first-born. It is a rare family who can have two first-borns working harmoniously together. More than likely there would be significant jockeying for first-born status until the pecking order was worked out. My guess is that if that was a real-life family one of the first-borns would have moved out as soon as they were physically and financially capable of doing so. The other siblings would have had similar teething problems with each trying to maintain the status and privileges that came with their original family positions. Imagine both youngest children vying for the status of the baby of the family! My bet is that the female later-born would win that position hands down.

Birth-order knowledge can help you get on better with your partner and help you to work together to raise your children. I believe in the notion that opposites attract and that they often make the best teams and partnerships. That's why first-borns who love to look after and care for others make great mates for youngest-borns who just love being taken care of. However it can be disconcerting living with someone who fundamentally has a different life view to you. It can be frustrating living with a cleanliness junkie (a first-born trait) if your idea of cleanliness and order is a quick wipe of the benches and a sweep of the floor once a fortnight (a later-born tendency). Or living with someone who puts chaos theory (second-born) into practice can be testing for someone who likes to plan his or her days in detail and not leave anything to chance (first-borns again). One partner may think that an event will never happen without elaborate planning, while the other may believe too much planning kills spontaneity. But as much as first-borns don't like uncertainty later-born partners can loosen this group up when they spring pleasant surprises on them. As much as they may not like surprises or feeling out of control first-borns actually benefit from some spontaneity in their lives. Birth-order knowledge helps partners understand each other, which is the first step toward working effectively together. There are no guarantees of success but as the following chapters will reveal there are many techniques to effectively raise, work with and live with people in each birth position.

Chapter 2

WHEN BIRTH ORDER DOESN'T MAKE SENSE

The influence your family has on you as you grow
up can reach across time and distance to touch you
in profound and sometimes disturbing ways years
after you think you've 'grown beyond all that'.

Kevin Leman

It is strange speaking about birth order to an audience. I usually receive two very different audience reactions as I discuss the typical characteristics of each position. One group of people will invariably nod their heads enthusiastically as they recognise themselves or their children in the descriptions I provide. People in this group typically tell me after a presentation that I must know their children personally so accurate is the picture I have constructed. Other people shake their heads or simply look confused at my explanation. 'Your description may be true of many children but it couldn't be further from the truth for my kids' is a common response. This doesn't mean that birth-order theory is not true for those families or people. There are many variables that influence birth order. Once these variables are understood and considered then it usually makes sense why some children don't fit a model or don't act according to expectation. No single factor determines a child's personality or behaviours. A whole range of factors work together to impact on a child's personality and birth order is just one of them. Understanding these various factors is the key to working out the effects of birth order on personality development.

It all happens within the family frame

It seems a quirk of nature that parents tend to focus on the differences between their children rather than the similarities. The differences can be a source of frustration to many parents struggling to understand their children's behaviour, interests and temperaments. One child may be academically oriented while the adjacent sibling shows little interest in schoolwork, regardless of their aptitude. Or one child may be the model of responsibility while another can't be relied upon to perform even the most basic tasks at home without at least three reminders. These differences are frustrating and tend to be amplified when a child behaves in ways that we consider inappropriate or that don't fit with the ideals we hold for the child.

Despite the differences which may be obvious children within a family have more in common than we think. When we focus on commonalities we begin to notice that children within a family generally share many personal characteristics and values. For instance, my three children at first glance appear very different but they share two dominant traits. They are fiercely independent and they are extremely assertive, all able to speak their minds when the opportunity arises. The children share these two traits because they reflect some dominant values of my family. As parents Sue and I have always encouraged the children to take risks, solve problems and to look after themselves and each other. *'Never regularly do for children the things they can do themselves'* has been a type of unspoken law in our family. Subsequently the children have grown up being able to fend for themselves in a vast range of ways. Also we have not minded if the children speak their mind as long as they choose the right forum and do so in a reasonable and respectful way. *'It is okay to speak up but you don't have to be rude or selfish about it'* is another unwritten family law. The values explicit in each family help to set the pattern for how children relate to each other and also how they behave in a whole range of circumstances.

The family provides the frame for children's development, and birth order provides the lens through which each child sees the world individually.

Family Frame = values + atmosphere + parenting style + relational style

The family frame sets the parameters for how a child in each position sees and experiences the world. The frame governs how children view the world and their relational style and its impact on their temperament. A family with a happy-go-lucky atmosphere provides a very different framework than a family with a hostile or very serious atmosphere. The oldest in a more relaxed family will still in all likelihood be the most responsible and serious child in the family but he or she will be far more relaxed than the first-born in a rigid, inflexible family. Similarly the youngest child in a family with very strict rules may still have more freedoms than elder siblings but he or she will have less freedom than the youngest child in a family with a laissez faire approach to limits and boundaries.

Your style of parenting influences how children interact with the world both in the present and the future. Each child has a particular lifestyle or view of the world that becomes their guiding principle as they respond to different situations and events. For instance, some children want to control everything, while others want to be the best at everything they do and some children go to great lengths to please others. When parenting is too strict or provides children with too much freedom, children can develop faulty lifestyles such as those mentioned above. The most appropriate parenting approach is one that strikes a balance between providing order and limits with freedom and opportunities to make choices. Anecdotal evidence suggests that this approach is most likely to promote a sense of personal confidence and generosity in children. Chapter 9 has more about lifestyle development and parenting style.

The way parents relate to each other and to their offspring impacts on children's current and future relational style. Some parents have very warm relationship styles characterised by open communication and a high degree of verbal and physical affection. At the other end of the spectrum is a cool style of relating, where emotional issues are avoided and affection is rarely shown. In reality most parents fall somewhere between the two extremes. Children will often pick up the same relational style as their same gender parent. So if a father shows his affection through play rather than in verbal ways it is likely that his sons will relate to others in the same way. If a mother is overtly affectionate then this becomes the model of relating for girls. An exception occurs when one parent has a style that overpowers all others so that everyone within the family relates to each other in that style. There is little doubt that the relational style of parents has a long-lasting impact on the way children relate to others.

Birth order is not just a neat set of numbers

In order to understand birth order it is important that you don't see it as simply a neat set of numbers. First-borns invariably behave in certain ways but sometimes second-borns act just like first-borns, and at times youngest children can seem like first-borns too. It is necessary to look at how children function rather than purely focus on their ordinal position. If a first-born acts more like a youngest then there is every chance that a second-born is functioning like a first-born within the family. If you're confused let's gain greater understanding by considering the variables that influence birth order.

Common variables impacting on birth order

Spacing

The age gap between siblings is perhaps the greatest variable influencing a child's birth order personality. Birth order is such a potent influence on children due to the competition between siblings for parental attention and approval. When the gap between siblings is two years or less then the rivalry is generally quite fierce. A sibling close in age can represent a threat, as they can be just as competent, just as smart and nearly as big as the elder child. For instance, there is nothing quite so threatening to a six year old who is supposed to be more capable than a four-year-old sibling who can recognise their own name, sound out letters and generally show how capable they are in the areas that parents value highly. The six year old will either have to keep the younger one in their place by showing others how clever he or she is or by pointing out the younger child's ineptitude both to the child and to the parents.

A mother told me how her five-year-old daughter brought home a painting from school and proudly displayed it beneath her chin for the whole family to see. Her seven-year-old brother gave it a quick once over and promptly remarked, 'You haven't used many colours. The dog is bigger than the people and you haven't filled up all the page.' The proud artist was crestfallen, as her brother didn't share her parents' enthusiasm. What in effect the eldest boy was saying to his sister was, 'You'll never be as good as me and don't ever forget it.' I have a hunch this younger sister had better get used to a picky older brother who will continually erode her efforts in areas that he values and she is perceived as a threat. This girl will probably become a little smarter over time about showing and discussing her schoolwork with her parents, choosing to do so in the absence of her elder sibling. She may even lose confidence and eventually interest in those areas where her brother continually puts her down.

The wider the age gap between two siblings the less likely there is to be competition. There is little point in a 10 year old competing with a four year old – the superiority is well established, unless there are unusual circumstances such as a long-term illness or disability.

These days families tend to be extremely well planned, with many parents opting for a gap of two or three years between children. This has the obvious advantage of all children in a family moving through each stage roughly together. In many ways life is easier to manage when children are of a similar age. The gap was big enough in my original family for my parents to be planning a wedding for my older sister while they were preparing me for my first day at school. That's quite a stretch for any parent. It is little wonder I recall that my parents always seemed to be tired and worn out. I learned that my mother would give in easily to my requests for a little extra freedom if I just applied a little pressure. A whine here, a nag there and Mum would give in without too much of a fight.

My own family was the result of better planning – with three children born within four years we have the advantage of all children moving through each life stage at the same time.

There has never been the problem of dropping one child off at kindergarten while driving another to university as occurs in some families. Management and lifestyle-wise, families with small age gaps may seem ideal but small gaps ensure one phenomenon – sibling rivalry.

My original family

Father – first of six children (both genders)

Mother – second of two children (both girls)

Female – 16

Female – 14

Male – 10

– – – – – – –

Male – 4

When there is a space of five or six years between siblings then the younger sibling often takes on the characteristics of a first-born. In many ways that child is beginning a new family, even if there is no-one else to follow. In my original family there are two distinct families – my three elder siblings above the line and yours truly below the line. If I hadn't come along it would have functioned like a fairly typical three-child family. My two sisters, like many firsts and seconds, are very different people. My brother would have fitted into the youngest mode but I came along and messed the whole lot up.

My family is interesting as in many ways there are three children with first-born tendencies. As there is such a large gap between my elder brother and myself I function very much like a first-born. Even though no-one followed I was in fact the eldest of the new family. As there was a significant gap between my brother and his sister he also functions like a first-born. When my sisters were around he was the youngest of the three, but when he was with me he was definitely my elder brother.

My parents gave him a great deal of the responsibility for looking after me, so he had to be a conscientious brother and a good role and gender model. He began work at a young age so I grew up almost as an only child. However my parents were well broken in by the time I came along so I had the easy, relaxed ride that many youngest children experience. I am a last-born child who carries many of the burdens of a first-born and I have many of the positive characteristics of the youngest, with few of the disadvantages that this group have. My brother is a third-born who functions more like a first-born than a middle or youngest as he was for six years. It is important to consider individual family circumstances when looking at the development of birth-order personalities.

Gender

Gender has a significant impact on children's personality due to biological and sociological reasons. Quite simply, the social-isation process is different for boys than for girls. Not only are boys and girls treated differently by parents and the commu-nity at large, within a family the arrival of a child of a different gender will trigger different responses and reactions according to the parental expectations and also to the gender of the other children. The long-awaited arrival of a girl after three boys will guarantee that she will receive different treatment than if the fourth child were another boy.

Gender needs to be considered when looking at the impact of birth order in my own family. In many ways I have two first-borns – my son and his adjacent sister. Sam is the pace-setter for the rest of the family and definitely wears the crown like most first-born boys. He knows he is the eldest and he likes to remind others of this fact. However Emma is the first of two girls so she has many first-born tendencies and also like many middle children is very flexible, with a well-developed set of social skills. If my second-born were a boy rather than a girl then that child would in all likelihood have been more like a second-born and the youngest would have been an only girl. A youngest child of a different gender to everyone has a very special place in the family. They are often spoiled and pampered due to their special position and there can be a great deal of resentment aimed at them from the sibling immediately above. The special child due to gender can place a great deal of pressure on children immediately above or below them.

The Grose family

Sue – second girl of five boys
Michael – youngest of four children
Sam – male 18
Emma – female 16
Sarah – female 14

Biology plays its part when it comes to the maturity gap between girls and boys. Frequently I see first-born boys with a second-born sister following close behind struggle to make the grade at school or even in sport. If the age gap is close then it may well be that developmentally there is very little difference between the two. First-borns like to keep a competency gap between them and the sibling that follows. There is nothing harder for a boy than to have a younger sister breathing down his neck as he tries to assert his superiority over her. It is no coincidence that I see many first-born boys who give up at school as they just can't compete with an equally or more competent younger sister. This seems to increasingly occur as families shrink in size and parents settle for the proverbial 'pigeon pair' of a boy and a girl.

Parenting expectations and birth position

Earlier I discussed the place that the family frame (consisting of the family atmosphere, parenting style and prominent values) plays in the development of a child's personality. It is within the family context that birth order impacts on children's personalities. One variable that we need to consider is a parent's own birth-order position. Parents often unconsciously identify, and have a strong affinity, with children of the same gender and also the same birth position. It is only in recent years that I have been aware of how strongly I identify with Sarah, the youngest daughter in my family. As her siblings' burgeoning social lives take them away from their family Sarah increasingly spends 'family time' on her own with her parents. As this is something I hated about being the youngest I have gone to great lengths to compensate for this new-found 'only-ness'. I have even insisted that she take friends along with us on outings so she doesn't feel alone. My reaction has been quite irrational and hasn't really matched the needs of the situation but it is typical of how strongly our own childhood experiences can influence our parenting. In many ways I have identified with my last-born in an indulgent way. Thankfully my even-handed second-born partner has intervened and helped me see sense.

The hypothetical family

Mother – first-born
Father – first-born
Male – 12
Female – 10
Male – 7

Look at the hypothetical family above and work out who has the favoured or even easiest position in the family. It is a toss-up between the female and the youngest male but my guess would be that the middle girl would have the most favoured position in the hypothetical family. Parents often identify most strongly with their same gender position and two first-born parents may well throw their hands up in despair at the laid-back attitude or even vagueness for which youngest-borns are renowned. The second-born would benefit from having her parents pour most of their high expectations into the first-born and may even benefit from having a low risk-taking, high-achieving elder sibling. The first-born boy in this family will probably have the most difficult time. This boy would probably have to live with pressure from two achievement-oriented first-borns who value organisation, which is not generally a boy's strong suit. The first-born boy will probably have his first bank account at birth, will be enrolled at a variety of schools by the end of his first year and will have his name put down for a number of clubs before he even learns to walk!

As family size decreases first-borns make up a greater percentage of the population. Currently just fewer than 50 per cent of children are first-born or only children. This is increasing at such a rapid rate that it has been estimated that in another 10 years close to 70 per cent of children will be first-borns. This will have a dramatic impact on all areas of life, including marriage, work and even parenting. Increasingly, more households will be headed by two first-borns who will invariably have their households running efficiently but I suspect will also head homes where anxiety, pressure and inflexibility are features of the family atmosphere.

Individual temperament

It is important to consider temperament when discussing the effects of birth order on kids. Temperament is often confused with personality but the two concepts are different. Temperament has a notion of permanence and is more closely related to biology than personality, which includes a broader range of attributes. The Australian Temperament Project distinguishes between temperament and personality (p 2): 'There are no clear ways of distinguishing between these terms [temperament and personality], but there is reasonable agreement that temperament more closely represents an inborn "style" of behaving, something which is observable in early childhood, well before an individual has had time to amass enough experience to have formed a personality.'

Children's temperament tends to remain similar throughout their lives, however it does modify according to their experiences. A child's temperament shapes the interactions that he or she has with others. A child with a shy temperament will interact quite differently with siblings than a child with an aggressive temperament. It seems that by the age of three or four the seeds are sown for good versus adverse adjustment. A child's temperament will influence how others react to the child. The Australian Temperament Project noted that adults tend to react more favourably to a child with a warmer positive temperament than they do to a child who possesses a negative, withdrawing temperament.

The study also uncovered evidence of a specific Australian temperament. It found that there is a tendency for Australian children to be a bit more laid-back, in the way that we expect, compared with children from many other countries. For example, the study found Italian toddlers were rather more volatile and excitable, compared with Australian children.

The study revealed that while children's temperaments changed they didn't change from one extreme to another over time. A shy child didn't become the most gregarious child in the class but that didn't mean that they didn't become less shy and more socially skilled. The results of the 18-year-old Australian

Temperament Project reveal, like numerous other studies of its type, that a child's development is a complex web of factors – both genetic and environmental. The genetic lottery throws up a certain temperament but the family and broader environment that it interacts with shape it. In many ways, it seems that a child's temperament is just potential waiting to be shaped.

Family circumstances – including death, adoption and blended families

Generally, the death of a child will affect birth-order influences in quite dramatic ways depending on the age and position of the child who passed away. If the eldest of two boys dies at around the age of 10 or 11 then the second-born suddenly becomes the eldest boy. He has been a second-born for so long he will find it more difficult to assume the mantle of first-born than if the death had happened at the age of three or four.

The surviving son has quite a burden to carry, particularly if the first-born was given plenty of responsibility and was a high achiever. The first-born has been the groundbreaker and in many ways the responsible eldest for 10 or so years. Now the second-born will, in all likelihood, feel the pressure of living in the shadow of a first-born who is generally idolised over time. It is no coincidence that most children who follow immediately after a sibling who has died generally experience some type of emotional, behavioural or learning problem. It is not easy to follow a sibling who never grows old and whose positive attributes are remembered long after their negative attributes are forgotten. Adults who have lost a sibling as a child frequently report that they felt as children that they *had to live two lives* – their own life and as standard-bearer for the sibling who passed away. In most cases they found that they could never live up to the memory of the dead sibling.

If in a family of three a first-born boy dies at the age of five, leaving behind a second-born sister and an infant baby brother then there is every chance that the girl will take over the first-born role and the baby brother will grow up as a first-born boy. He will probably take on many attributes of his brother, depending on what role his sister fills. The death of a sibling at a young age affects the way parents raise and view the surviving children. They are frequently and quite naturally seen as 'special jewels' and overprotected, which is very common in small families. This is natural as parents will do everything in their power to protect their surviving children and won't allow them to take what are seen as normal risks.

Adoption doesn't affect birth order if it happens when the child adopted is a baby or toddler-aged. However if parents adopt a child who is five years old or more then the child has more than likely established his or her birth-order personality. A child who has been brought up as a youngest won't necessarily act like a first-born if adopted into a family as the first or a single child. It is not wise family politics to adopt a child who is older than natural children. Your natural first-born will in all likelihood not take too kindly to being knocked off his or her perch and will resent the intruder. As a rule children resent being replaced or moved one place back in the pecking order. They usually don't mind if a child is placed below them as this reinforces their position, unless they have been replaced as the baby of the family. Some children don't take too kindly to losing this special position.

A consequence of our current high divorce rate is the rise in the phenomenon of the blending of two families. Why a phenomenon? Well, it is a wonder that these families survive at all. Two families joining together don't so much blend as collide. Blended families don't operate like intact families. The norms and rules that govern family life are different for blended families than they are for intact families. Blended families by their nature are born out of the loss of an original family. Resentment, divided loyalty, betrayal of an original parent and an unwillingness to let go of their original family are just some of the elements that blended families share. Parents in blended families have a longer relationship with their own children than they have with their new partner so parental loyalty is generally severely tested over partner loyalty.

If families blend when children are very young then family life is often less contentious and less complicated. But if children are predominantly over five and their birth-order personalities are established then the step-parents can be assured that they will be in for some rocky times. It is important to remember that children's birth-order personalities are formed by the age of five or six and are unlikely to change after that. Birth-order personality can modify, can alter and can adapt to suit different circumstances but it is unlikely to change much after that age. Once a first-born always a first-born and so it goes for each subsequent position.

Kevin Leman in *The New Birth Order Book* states emphatically (p. 61), 'Blended families do not create new birth-order positions. Because one first-born suddenly has a stepbrother or sister who is older, that doesn't mean that the first-born stops being typically conscientious, structured, well organised, or perfectionist. By the same token, a last-born isn't suddenly going to change his personality because a divorce and remarriage make him a middle child in the family. He'll still lean toward being a show-off, an attention-seeker, a manipulator (and), a charmer . . .'

The imaginary blended family

Mother (only)	Father (first-born)
Male – 13	Male – 15
Male – 11	Female – 13
Female – 8	

If you were a child in the imaginary blended family which position would you prefer to be in? Which position is the least attractive? The two first-born boys would have an interesting time in their duel for sibling supremacy, especially if they both had aggressive temperaments. Unless the mother's first-born son has a particularly strong or even aggressive personality and the father's first-born was fairly timid, which is highly unlikely with a first-born father, then the first-born male would rule the sibling roost. The mother's second son is in the unenviable position of not only playing second fiddle to his natural brother but he has a second-born stepsister who is two years older than him. He has been pushed down the pecking order two notches, which is not something he would be thrilled about. I imagine he would be very much like many typical middle children – he would like to get even. He may either be uncooperative with his older siblings or be extremely bossy to his younger sister, assuming the role of eldest to this step-sibling. Unfortunately, he probably hasn't the perks that go with being the first-born nor the experience of being responsible. The mother's youngest daughter may be in the favoured position in this family. She hasn't been displaced so she is still the youngest in the family with four rather than two elder siblings to charm, manipulate and put in her service. However there is one variable that could upset this idyllic position – her mother. If her mother, who was a 'special jewel' as an only child herself, saw her daughter in this light then she has lost her only female child status now that her stepsister has come along. She may not have lost her youngest position but she has lost her unique-ness that goes with being the only child of a particular gender, which is intensified by being the youngest.

Blended families may not create new birth-order positions but they certainly are one of the variables in the mix that creates unique individuals. A child's position in the family alone will not be the cause or even sole predictor of the child's personality and behaviour. But when you understand birth-order theory and consider the variables that impact on it in any given circumstance then you can gain a clearer picture of why a person behaves as they do and why they have turned out the way they have.

Special-needs children

When a child is born with a disability or is chronically ill then the most common result is that he or she becomes a functional youngest, regardless of the birth position. The severity and nature of the illness or disability as well as parents' reaction are two factors that impact on the child's personality development relative to his or her birth-order position. If parents react positively to the disability and treat them as they would any other child then they are more likely to develop typical characteristics of their birth position.

This was the case with the Minchin family whose eldest son Paul was born blind over 50 years ago. With eight siblings following in a little over 15 years, Paul's parents were not in a position to protect or spoil their first-born. When you consider that twin girls came along next, Paul's mother had her hands full so there would have been little opportunity for her to mollycoddle her son. As a result Paul, like many first-borns, became independent at a relatively early age. Although he wasn't given the usual responsibilities of looking after younger siblings like many eldest children Paul still enjoyed many of the perks and disadvantages that first-borns experience. He carried head of the family status as he was the first to get a paid job and he was the first child to marry and have a family. He also has an extraordinarily determined streak, which helped him overcome any obstacles that stood in the way of his independence. More than once when he was in his late teens he overshot his train stop, which added over two hours to his train trip home from work. He took such challenges in his stride and considered them part of everyday life.

This situation contrasts significantly to that experienced in the Tower family. The first-born girl was born with severe intellectual disabilities so the child next in line functioned like a first-born. The first-born girl effectively became the youngest with the next two children taking a step up in position. Thomas, the second-born, learned early about responsibility. As an adult he recalled that as a young boy his mother took on the task of feeding, bathing and caring for his sister, which was almost a full-time job in itself. Thomas, in turn, became a substitute parent to his younger brother. Due to the severity of the disability, Thomas and his youngest brother were constantly aware that they needed to be careful around their sister. So the horseplay that is so often a part of children's early life was out of the question. Thomas's overdeveloped sense of caution and responsibility is still a feature of his personality 40 years later.

The next child in line is usually the most severely affected by a disability or illness as parents generally expect them to fill in that sibling's position role. As in Thomas's case they tend to take on more of the caretaking role for other children when a child is born with a disability.

Functioning like another position

Often people function like someone born in a certain position even though they were born in a different position. For instance, many people function like first-borns even though they may have been born second or further down the family tree. I have found that there is usually an explanation for a person acting more like someone in another birth position. A friend who heard me speak about birth order at a dinner party said I was talking a load of rubbish. She was the second-born in her family of four children and she was precisely like the first-born I had just described. She claimed that she had always been the boss in her family and now as an adult she was responsible for keeping her siblings together. She organised family functions and she had power of attorney for her ailing elderly mother. After a little probing I discovered that it made perfect sense that she act like a first-born. Her elder sister, who preceded her by two years, was born with one lung and subsequently was a passive, even protected child. She spent considerable time in hospital through illness as a child so her younger sibling effectively took over her role as elder statesperson of the siblings to come. Her parents looked to her to be the voice for her family at school and to take many family responsibilities around the home, even acting as baby-sitter to younger children while in her early teens. My dinner party friend may have been born second but she functioned like a first-born from very early in life.

Leapfrogging

Sometimes children in families will swap roles or leapfrog positions. This more commonly occurs between first- and second-born children, although it can happen with a youngest jumping up a notch. I saw this phenomenon occur in my family, as my first- and second-born children leapfrogged each other in early adolescence. Sam, my first-born, was very typical of many first-born boys – he had a serious attitude to life (he was dubbed 'Serious Sam'), he was conscientious and he was a low risk taker. He hated to stand out in a crowd, preferring to stay in the background and avoid being noticed. I remember him standing shyly in the background dressed as one of the three wise men in a nativity play at his preschool. Standing way in the background on the stage was enough involvement for this shy young first-born. Preschool and school for Sam were places of learning rather than socialising. His second-born sister, Emma, was just the opposite when she was young. Emma had a laid-back, relaxed attitude to life (she was dubbed 'Easy-going Emma'). As a youngster she wouldn't miss any activity – life was something you participated in rather than observed. Primary school for her was a place where you went to meet your friends. She worked hard but this wasn't her prime objective. While Sam was serious, Emma was relaxed. While Sam was reserved, Emma was adventurous (with a number of trips to hospital outpatients as proof). While Sam was interested in art, Emma was inter-ested in sport. Sometime around the age of Sam's 14th birthday Emma became more like a first-born and her brother didn't so much function like a second-born but functioned in ways that Emma didn't. Sam became less interested in school and more interested in social and creative aspects of life. He loosened up and took a far more relaxed, laid-back approach to life, refusing to get too anxious over little things like incomplete homework or missing assignments. At the same time his sister assumed a great deal of responsibility for helping out at home and also took a far more serious, studious approach to her schoolwork. Emma leapfrogged over Sam and Sam didn't mind one little bit losing the mantle of first-born.

Now they function more like two first-borns, which is quite common for that particular gender mix (more about this in Chapter 10). For now it is useful to remember that sometimes one child will leapfrog over another and assume the position of the sibling above. When this happens the eldest may still func-tion in some ways as their birth position suggests but in other ways they adopt the birth-order personality of the sibling who has taken their position.

Multiple births

Twins, like single children, are on the increase. The likelihood of giving birth to twins increases as a mother gets older. The frequency of one set of twins every 90 births, which is the rate for white people, will increase as women delay the birth of their first child and with the increase in the use of fertility drugs to assist conception. In the past the majority of twins were youngest-born, as women in their 40s are twice as likely to give birth to twins as women in their 20s. With women delaying the birth of their first child it is becoming more likely for twins to be born first than in any other position.

If there are no siblings then twins are more likely to behave typically like any first- and second-borns. They will be different from each other in temperament, interests and even their strengths; nevertheless the differences won't be as strong as other firsts and seconds. Most children are keen to put as much distance between their siblings and themselves in terms of interests, strengths and personality as they can, but twins can feel uncomfortable with too much difference.

In some circumstances, twins will alternate between first-born and youngest. One twin may take the lead in the area of games, play and social situations, while the other may dominate in academic proceedings. If parents emphasise one sibling over another or look to the child born first as being the eldest then one child may be the 'dominant' twin. When twins are born last in the family as they most commonly have been, then they have the dubious honour of being both the youngest and having the notoriety of being a twin. Regardless of where they come in the family twins act like first and second with each other. As Kevin Leman writes in *The New Birth Order Book* (p. 47) 'No matter where twins may land in a family birth order, they wind up as something of a first-born/second-born combination and are usually competitor and companion. The first-born often becomes the assertive leader and the second-born follows along.'

Twins experience a parenting style and a family situation that few other children experience. As parents have to split themselves between two children twins frequently don't have such strong ties to their parents as other children share. Before they begin school twins spend almost all their time together so their greatest influence is on each other. The relationship between twins themselves may be intense but they experience many of the advantages and disadvantages of youngest children, regardless of their position. They certainly experience less parental anxiety and pressure. As Richardson and Richardson explain in *Birth Order and You* (p. 188), 'Twins also usually have less parental pressure to achieve than other children. Parents just don't have as much time to worry over every little thing and measure progress in the same way.'

Also as their parents are frequently tired they tend to experience more inconsistent discipline than other children. They have the advantage of being able to gang up on their mother and find that it is easy to ignore parental commands unless they are addressed individually. Twins are less worried about parental approval and they don't pay as much attention to parents and teachers as other children. So twins who are first-born may be responsible but less concerned about preserving the status quo and deferring to authority than other first-borns.

It is not easy being a sibling to multiples

A multiple birth can place pressure on those born immediately before and immediately after the big event. If you are the youngest in the family but follow twins then it would be hard to compete for attention with a double act. The specialness of being youngest would be lost amongst the noise and fuss surrounding the twins. This is heightened when all children are the same gender. Take a look at the Harris family and work out who is in the most unfavourable position:

The Harris family

Male - 18

Male −15

Male −15

Male −13

The youngest boy has a real battle on his hands to be noticed. The first-born boy, like many first-born males, rules the roost. He excels at sport and is a high achiever at school. The twin boys tend to dominate family proceedings. They both excel at sport – not in the same sport – and they both have heavy schedules of active extra-curricular activities. The parents are busy following the sporting and extra-curricular exploits of their two middle sons. It is hard for the youngest male to stand out amongst this high achieving, noisy group, which is exacerbated by the fuss and bother that everyone from grandparents through to neighbours make of 'the twins'. Subsequently, the youngest boy has chosen the 'clown' route to get some attention. He has chosen not to go head to head with his twin brothers and excel at sport or even perform well at school. Rather he spends much of his time being, in his parents' words, the 'family fool' and 'class clown'. His parents are at their wits' ends trying to make sure their youngest toes the line but they have a discouraged child on their hands who just can't compete with the double act up the line.

I am an individual

One of the keys to helping twins develop their own personalities is for parents and other adults such as teachers and grandparents to treat them as individuals who share the same birthday, rather than as 'twins'. This means that parents dress them differently, buy separate birthday presents and address them by their names rather than referring to them as 'the twins'. If possible give them separate bedrooms although this may not happen until they are well into their primary school years. It is not always easy for parents to treat their multiples as individuals. You may try to treat them as individuals however you may find that everyone from the nurse who helped deliver them through to the principal at their primary school refers to them as 'the twins'. As for dressing them as individuals it can be a nightmare buying a different set of clothes for two children at once. And many twins refuse point blank to have a bedroom of their own, opting to share with their sibling as long as they can.

It is important for parents not to label either twin because not only are you giving a twin a name to live up to but you are assigning a different role to the other twin. For instance, if you refer to one twin as the 'academic' one or the 'smart' one there is every chance that the other twin will not tread down the academic path with as much gusto as the other twin. Why would the twin when he or she is not the smart one?

One, two, three . . . four

Multiple births tend to skew birth-order positions. There is very little research available on the subject of birth order and triplets (and more), however anecdotal research suggests that three children would take on a family constellation all of their own. In other words, giving birth to triplets would be like having a firstborn, a second and a youngest, all born on the same day. One very busy mother I know with three delightful five-year-old girls sits back in fascination and watches her children play out the three birth-order roles. It is not surprising as the nature of groups means that if three children spent enough time together they would eventually take on characteristics of the three different birth-order positions. One child would tend to be the bossy first-born, while one child would, in all likelihood, begin to charm and put the other children in his or her service and the other child would be squeezed between a charmer and a boss and learn to either get along or separate him or herself from the group, which is a second-born characteristic. There are many variables at play, including temperament, gender and parenting style however birth-order theory plays itself out in fascinating ways when multiples enter the picture.

It is how you function that counts

In many respects birth-order personality relates to how a person functions rather than the actual position they take in the family. Alfred Adler, the father of birth-order theory, says that children cannot be understood in isolation. He maintained that our behaviour only makes sense when you understand the context of the social environment in which it occurs. In the same way, to understand a person's birth-order personality it is important to look at the variables at play, which are usually hard to glean at first glance. But if you know a little about a person's family background then you can begin to make some intelligent guesses that may begin to explain why a person diverges from the usual personality traits for their position.

Recently I worked with someone who functions like a first-born but actually comes last in her family. So strong were the first-born tendencies toward perfectionism, achievement and goal setting that I was surprised to find that she was the youngest of three. My first guess was that there was a large gap between herself and her siblings. Bingo! She was youngest in the family but there was a 10 year gap between her and her adjacent sibling.

This large gap meant that she was the first-born of her new family but she was never displaced. She would have had some experiences in common with youngest children but she would have experienced a life more in common with a super first-born – an only or single child.

Chapter 3

FIRST-BORNS FORGE AHEAD – LEADERSHIP MATERIAL OR NEUROTIC PERFECTIONISTS?

The oldest child – the first child – is like a first love.
The relationship between the first child and
parents can never be duplicated.
Ronald W. Richardson & Lois A. Richardson

We had all better get used to living with first-borns because eldest-born children are everywhere and the numbers are increasing astronomically. If you are reading this book there is close to 50 per cent probability that you are a first-born. If you have a partner there is a similar probability that he or she will be an eldest. You will find that between 40 to 50 per cent of those people at work, in your groups of friends and at your leisure or sports clubs, will be first-borns. When you add to this the number of functional first-borns – that is, those people who due to family circumstances function like first-borns – then the number increases dramatically.

If you are a teacher or involved in a professional capacity with children then approximately five out of every 10 children you come into contact with will be first-born. The proportion of first-borns increases as families shrink in size and families are shrinking in Western countries like Australia at a rapid rate so there will be more first-borns proportionate to the rest of the population in the future.

Percentage of numbers of children under the age of eighteen for Australian mothers

17.35 per cent of women have one child

37.61 per cent of women have two children

25.22 per cent of women have three children

19.83 per cent of women have four or more children

(ABS figures, June 2002)

The increase in the proportion of first-borns has huge ramifications for the community. Some commentators have suggested that a person standing for politics over the coming decades would stand a better chance of election if he or she stood on the conservative side due to the higher proportion of first-borns. He reasons that due to the inherently conservative nature of this birth-order group they will be more likely to stick to the status quo when they cast their votes. This is a reasonable proposition given what we know about first-borns.

What are first-borns really like?

There is more written about first-borns than any other position presumably because there are more of them. The work of Frank Sulloway and many other researchers shows that first-borns share many of the same characteristics.

Characteristics of first-borns

First-borns tend to be:
- goal-setters
- high achievers
- perfectionists
- responsible
- rule keepers
- determined
- detail people.

First-borns tend to be highly organised. They are list makers who love systems of any type. If you want someone to develop and maintain your office filing system, your financial control system, or your marketing system, then choose an eldest. They were born for it. This group gravitates towards jobs where attention to detail and precision are required. They are generally more conscientious about their work than those from many other positions and they love to set goals. Next time someone talks in terms of the short and long-term goals they have set for any aspect of their life check their birth order. There is every chance that they will be first-borns as this group love to have something to work toward and love to do so in an orderly way. The motto for this group is: *life needs a purpose.*

First-borns are renowned as high achievers because they are more motivated to achieve than later-borns. Obviously many factors impact on the type of job a person chooses however it is no coincidence that a greater percentage of first-borns end up in professions such as medicine, accounting and the law. These professions not only have relatively high status, which first-borns value highly, but they are professions where determination, strong powers of concentration and discipline are required. These are qualities that are linked with first-borns. First-borns tend to end up in leadership positions whether they want to or not. Experiences in their family of origin provide terrific leadership training for eldest children, who are generally given plenty of responsibility at a young age. Significantly, over 50 per cent of US presidents and Australian prime ministers were first-borns, which is all the more remarkable as families were far larger in the past, decreasing the statistical chance of being a first-born. Quite simply there were less of them around in past years.

In seminars I ask the first-borns in the room to stand as I describe their characteristics. Their faces beam at the favourable description they hear because achievement-oriented first-borns want recognition. It's true that all people love recognition for their achievements but first-borns thrive on it. If you are looking for a way to motivate a first-born then make sure you give them some recognition for their good work, their good manners or their efforts. It helps if you make the recognition public. Praise a first-born in front of his or her workmates for completing a project on time and you can guarantee that they will complete the next project well ahead of time. Praise a child for doing great schoolwork in front of his or her peers and you know they will keep up the intensity of their efforts. (Parents need to be careful about praising first-borns too publicly at home as this can fuel intense competition with siblings, but that is another story dealt with in Chapter 10.) First-borns love recognition. Ironically parents so often find it difficult to give them the recognition they crave.

Some first-borns are given huge amounts of responsibility. The following account shows just how much responsibility first-borns can assume:

I am 35 years old and the eldest of three children. I have a sister two years younger and a brother seven years younger than me.

My upbringing was not ideal. My mother didn't cope very well with things and was an alcoholic. My father coped with this by not being very involved with us. To the best of my knowledge, this started around the time my brother was born. Dad didn't come home for nights and was not very reliable. I always had to get lifts from friends 'because he was working'. Things were violent occasionally; there was lots of verbal abuse and I felt that my parents didn't relate to us. I feel that this has affected me differently to my brother and sister, because I am the eldest. I was older and therefore tend to remember what happened and I believe that in many aspects I became the adult in the house. I used to step in and take care of my brother and sister when Mum said she was leaving. I would cook dinner, clean up and comfort them (Sharen Job).

There are costs of being a first-born

Hard-driven first-borns can pay a high price for their achievements. They are often more neurotic, more intense and more inflexible than any other birth position. And according to a recent study they are more likely to develop heart disease than any other group, as they are more prone to experiencing stress.

But let's look at how firsts become so serious, so intense, so responsible and so conservative.

The first-born's arrival is a huge event

If you are a parent you will recall that the birth of your first child was a huge event for you and your broader family. If you have other children you may remember that the birth of your first child was different to the others. The build-up to the birth was probably longer and more exciting than the lead-up to subsequent births. There is every chance that early in the pregnancy you began to leaf through name books checking out possible names. You probably had a number of ultrascans with your partner in attendance. Knowing that preparation was important you probably attended numerous antenatal classes to learn all you could about the coming birth. Recently a friend announced that she was pregnant. After congratulating her I couldn't resist asking if she had been to antenatal classes yet. She proudly announced that she had been to one class and that she was attending a two-day live-in program the following weekend. That's dedication for you!

If you were like many parents you began preparing a nursery well before the birth and obtained a huge supply of baby clothes and nappies. There was an air of expectancy in your home that was almost tangible.

The birth itself of the first-born is a life-changing event. Every parent knows that their lives will be forever changed by the new life that they hold. Such was the excitement and the emotion surrounding the birth of the first-born that you didn't realise that the baby you were bringing home was actually an experiment or, to be more accurate, a groundbreaker. Not only did he or she break you in for any subsequent siblings but they introduced you to all the stages of development from infancy through to adolescence. It is through your eldest that you as a parent experienced playgroups, kindergartens, primary school and secondary school for the first time. It is your firstborn who introduces you to many common childhood issues and dilemmas such as tantrums, night fears and bedtime hassles.

It is often first-borns who cause parents to buy parenting books and attend parenting seminars. For a little fun I sometimes ask parents at my seminars to raise their hand if they have come along primarily to learn something that will help them with their first-born. The response is amazing as the majority of the audience raise their hands, albeit feeling a little sheepish that their true intention has been uncovered.

It is with your eldest that you first deal with typical adolescent issues such as going to parties, sexuality, drugs and alcohol usage, that really test your tolerance levels and your negotiating skills. Parents of first-borns tend to learn a great deal on the run. Some first-borns take advantage of parents' inexperience and learn to get their own way but first-borns commonly complain that their parents give them less latitude than younger siblings. Anecdotal evidence suggests that many parents are far stricter on their first-born children than they are on subsequent children. In my original family I was given the run of the house compared to my siblings. As a young child I saw first-hand many severe arguments that my parents had with my siblings over issues such as the right to drink alcohol and suitable times to come home from an evening out. But there were few battles by the time I reached adolescence because I was granted twice as much personal freedom as my siblings. As I said earlier my mother was a little tired and battle-fatigued by the time I came along and she was also more astute at choosing the battles to engage in. Experience had taught her which battles were important and worth making a stand over and which were trivial and worth ignoring.

Parents of first-borns can overdo it

Parents of first-born children have a tendency to overdo things. Everything a first-born child does is recorded for posterity either on photographs or on video. Contrast this with a youngest-born, where they are lucky to find a photo of themselves on their own should they scrounge through the photo albums at some later date. Parents measure, dissect and record every aspect of their first-born child's physical, social and intellectual development.

They compare their child's developmental rate with other children's rates and worry if their child is a little behind developmentally. They are aware of the age when their eldest first walked, talked and began to read. The crèche, preschool, primary school and secondary school you choose for the first child will invariably set the pattern for children to follow. Many parents begin investment funds, take out insurance policies, and put names down for private schools and clubs at the birth of the first-born. This zeal is often watered down by the time a third or fourth child arrives as parents are too busy.

First-born children are born into a privileged position. Living in the spotlight they generally get piles of attention from parents, grandparents and a host of other relatives and family friends. As they grow up they are given more responsibility than children in other positions and so they enjoy an almost regal status in most families. They lead the way, break new ground and rule the roost if others follow. The flipside for first-borns is that they tend to live with pressure. The expectations on first-borns to perform and live up to the family name is immense. When I ask parents what they want their children to be like, no-one ever says that they want them to be a lawyer, sports star or earn great wealth. I get responses like: 'I don't care what she does as long as she is happy and is a caring person' or 'Really, it is up to him what he becomes. I just want to him to reach his full potential' or 'As long as he is a decent human being and he tries his best at whatever he does then I won't mind'. These types of comments are nothing more than self-deception. Most people actually believe what they are saying but somewhere deep down most parents have high hopes and great dreams for their children. Whether we want our children to achieve in areas where we didn't or we just want out children to be a better and smarter version of ourselves most parents have big aspirations for their offspring. We are just unaware of it at a conscious level. These aspirations unwittingly fall onto the shoulders of their first-borns and they become the burden that first-borns carry. It helps if parents have a number of children as the hopes and dreams are spread among many children and don't become the burden of one or two children.

First-borns spend more of their early time around adults and learn more from adults than subsequent children in the family. Perhaps this is one reason why firstborns tend to score better on achievement and self-esteem tests than children in other positions. Certainly spending more time around parents assists their language development as the interaction during one-on-one time with a first-born lends itself to high quality language development. First-borns are less likely to be influenced by the behaviour of siblings and more likely to be influenced by their parents than children born in any other position.

Parents generally expect far too much of first-borns. In fact, the expectations can be so high that many first-borns, particularly boys, are afraid of making mistakes and errors of any kind. As they don't want to disappoint their parents or let them down many first-borns take the easy track as learners and avoid taking risks of any kind. I have taught first-borns who avoid using large words when they write for fear of making spelling errors. They preferred to write in stilted language rather than stretch their vocabulary and make a few mistakes in the process. First-borns generally like to be in the spotlight only if they can be the stars. They will stay away from the spotlight if they risk making a mistake, which may shatter the star image.

The curse of perfectionism

Many first-borns are afflicted by the curse of perfectionism. It may seem strange to say it but first-borns need to make more mistakes. We should encourage our kids to make more errors, spell more words incorrectly, get more sums wrong, make a mess sometimes when they write, break a dish or two as they unpack the dishwasher, set the table with the knife and fork upside down, leave marks on the floor when they wipe up the mess or forget to feed the cat once a in while. Children benefit from being released from the pressure of having to do well all the time. When children learn that mistakes are quite acceptable they are more likely to stretch themselves and try new areas of endeavour or use their own initiative and not worry if they mess up.

Perfectionism is a modern curse in many of our schools. I conduct leadership programs with very capable 11 and 12 year olds and I am constantly surprised by their unwillingness to take risks or even take the initiative lest they be seen as making a mistake. Fear of making mistakes holds back more children and is a greater impediment to children reaching their full potential than any school-funding issue that tends to make front-page news from time to time. It is not lack of ability, opportunity or even laziness that holds many kids back. Rather it is a deep-seated unwillingness to expose themselves as temporary failures while they learn that stops them from really achieving their full potential. This fear of failure is strongest amongst first-borns, our most prolific population cohort, so it is little wonder that perfectionism is one of our greatest problems in Australian schools.

The burden of responsibility and the curse of perfectionism that first-borns carry means that first-borns will only star or achieve in areas where they are certain of success. So they tend to narrow their options by sticking to the safest path. It is little wonder that this group tends to be less innovative and adventurous than later-born children. The road to innovation and adventure is also littered with uncertainty, which increases the likelihood of making errors.

Perfectionists are hard to live with. They make demanding partners and anxious children. They can be critical of those around them just as they are highly critical of themselves. Their attention to detail can be infuriating. Their inflexibility can be enraging particularly if you are an easy-going second or middle child. Perfectionists usually want to be better than anyone else. You can pick a perfectionist at 1000 metres.

Following are some behaviours that are characteristic of perfectionists:

- *Perfectionists plan everything* – They won't go on a family picnic unless the route is known beforehand, the estimated time of arrival is decided upon and the weather is checked out days before. Perfectionists like to be in control so they don't leave things to chance.

- *Perfectionists are neurotic about order* – Tidy desks, shoes neatly arranged in wardrobes and neatly stacked food shelves are de rigueur for perfectionists.

- *Perfectionists are critical of themselves and others* – If a perfectionist paints a room he or she will focus on the inevitable thin spot rather than celebrate a job very well done. Consequently they don't enjoy success.

- *Perfectionists hate to leave jobs half done* – They will stay at work until a task is completed.

- *Perfectionists procrastinate* – Many perfectionists put off starting projects because they doubt if they can do them perfectly. Procrastination is not just a great stalling tactic, it is a protective strategy. They wait until conditions are perfect to start a job. The trouble is the time is never perfect so they never start.

- *Perfectionists don't like to delegate* – No-one but no-one can do a job as well as they can so they tend to take on far too much and they don't trust anyone to do a task as well as they can.

- *Perfectionists apologise a lot* – They will always find an excuse such as there is not enough time or money to do the job that they would like. Perfectionists always believe that they can do better or try harder.

- *Perfectionists don't expect success* – They are generally pessimistic and look for reasons not to do things rather than reasons to try things. Their expectations become a self-fulfilling prophecy.
- *Perfectionists are governed by absolutes* – They see the world as black and white and have strong opinions about what people should and should not do.

How to help perfectionists

Many of you will be thinking that I am taking this perfectionism stuff a bit far. Or maybe you think that I am promoting shoddy workmanship or poor service. Like anyone else I value a job well done. I expect my car to be properly serviced when it goes into the garage and expect the mechanic to do a first-class job when adjusting my brakes. One of my hobbies is scuba diving and I expect that my tanks will be filled with the correct amount of oxygen. In fact, when I sit 18 metres below the surface of the water I depend on good workmanship. There are few margins for error in some circumstances. I expect condom-makers and parachute-makers to do a perfect job. But not every task requires perfectionism. Sometimes near enough is good enough, particularly if you are trying new endeavours. Writing a story, painting a house, cooking a meal or playing a game of golf have healthy margins for error. The trouble with some people is that they believe that they only count in the eyes of others when they are perfect, look perfect, or can do the perfect job. These people need to learn that just doing a good job of anything is acceptable.

The great psychologist Rudolph Dreikurs talked about the 'courage to be imperfect'. He believed that people are motivated by either of two forces: the desire to be superior or better than others, or the desire to contribute or be useful. Those motivated by the first force are never content because there will always be someone who can do a better job. Those motivated by the latter find contentment and fulfilment not only because their contributions usually assist others but also because they are not obsessed by doing a perfect or terrific job. Their satisfaction comes from helping not from achievement. Currently our society promotes perfectionism. It is rampant so it is no surprise that most people are motivated by the first force.

Dreikurs said:

> *We have to . . . realise that we are good enough as we are — because we never will be better, regardless of how much we may know, how much more skill we may acquire, how much more status or money or what-have-you.*

Dreikurs maintains that we have to accept our faults and don't put pressure on ourselves to be superhuman or be better than others. When we focus our efforts on the contribution that we make rather than on doing the perfect job then we live happy and more fulfilled lives and, ironically, we grow more capable as individuals.

I agree with Kevin Leman, the author of *The New Birth Order Book*, who claims that perfectionists need to learn to be satisfied with excellence, rather than perfectionism. Now excellence is pretty good. I am not suggesting that they should always settle for second-best efforts. They need to lower the bar a little and be more realistic about what they can achieve. I worked with a young teacher who was afflicted by perfectionism. She was a terrific educator with textbook techniques but her biggest problem was her inability to adapt to different teaching methods unless she could be absolutely perfect. When a person learns any new skill they usually spend some amount of time at the incompetent end of the learning curve. Some of the new teaching strategies required in the 1980s and 1990s, including those linked with information technology, meant that many teachers themselves had to go back to basics and in many cases, start all over again. Many of my teaching colleagues became learners themselves but my perfectionist colleague refused to budge and adopt new methods of teaching. She was branded as stubborn and lazy. But she was neither of these. She was such a perfectionist that she was scared to go back to school and make a whole heap of mistakes while she learned and implemented new teaching strategies. Many teachers who grasped new methods in the late 1990s found that they floundered for a while, but most persevered and have become better teachers for it. The pity is that her colleagues and peers have left behind my colleague. I have observed her and I know she teaches beautifully using some great techniques but she is no longer an excellent teacher. She is teaching children using methodology that is at least 30 years old. She needed to be happy with just being excellent, even pretty good for a while, but she placed such high expectations on herself that she didn't grant herself permission to mess up. Being a slave to perfectionism means that people become observers rather than participants in many aspects of life, whether at work or in their leisure time. They tend to look on as others get on with what is required of them.

Three types of first-borns

It is fascinating to look at how first-borns score in personality tests. My hunch is that they would score highly as Type A hard-drivers, directors and controllers depending on what type of test is used. From observation first-borns and functional first-borns can be placed into three distinct types:

1. The leader of the pack
2. The shepherd (second mother or father)
3. The hard-driver (high octane superwoman/man).

Leader of the pack

It is not so much that first-borns are born leaders but rather that leadership and responsibility are often thrust upon them. I recall Terry, my best friend from my boyhood, always had to look after his younger brother. Invariably his younger brother would tag along when we played together. His mother insisted that Terry either stay home to keep his brother occupied or let him tag along. Terry was given a responsibility that he didn't want and that none of his siblings were given. It is little wonder that first-borns tend to be found in leadership positions of all kinds. Responsibility of some kind is generally given to them at an early age.

But first-borns don't necessarily make great leaders. Many first-borns confuse assertiveness with aggression and gain cooperation through coercion. In my work with student leaders I find many first-born boys who confuse leadership with bossiness. They must have their own way and have difficulty conceding ground or seeing that there is any other way of doing things than their own way. These children like to be leaders of the pack and do so successfully as long as everyone else is willing to go along with their ideas. These first-borns like to be in charge and have difficulty filling any position other than a managerial or leadership role. One classic example of a leader of the pack was Donna, a lovely lady who was on a committee that I chaired some years back. As chairman, I led the group through an agenda at our meetings but Donna would inevitably railroad it. Whenever an issue was discussed Donna would have the first say and also the last. She would remind me when it was time to discuss a new point or when anyone was out of order. At first I was taken aback by her attempts to run the meetings and dominate the discussions. She wasn't nasty or trying to unseat me, she just wasn't used to being part of a group where she wasn't in charge. Being part of a team meant one thing to Donna – taking the lead. I gave Donna the chance to put her leadership skills to good use by giving her some projects to drive and complete. She completed them like a leader of the pack – efficiently, effectively, but with little delegation.

The shepherd (second mother or father)

One feature that many first-borns share is that many of them just love to please others. They love to please because they have a strong need for the approval of others. At first it is their parents' approval they strive for and later they seek approval of other authority figures such as relatives, teachers, coaches and bosses. They learned as children that one sure way to please their parents is to be compliant model children who do well at school and in areas that their parents' value. If a father excelled at sport then there is every chance that his first-born son will also try to excel on the sporting field. Often first-born girls become nurturing caregivers just like their mothers, particularly if there are two or three younger siblings to care for. It is not so much that these children become 'chips off the old block' and become copies of their parents, just that in trying to please their parents they act and behave like them.

Thankfully for this group they reach adolescence and pleasing their parents plays second fiddle to pleasing their peers. Some young people can succumb to peer pressure and engage in dangerous risk-taking behaviour, however for most healthy adolescents this is not the case. It is normal for young people to experiment with a range of behaviours that they know would meet with their parents' disapproval if they ever found out. Even then these compliant first-borns tend to tiptoe around the fringes rather than jump, feet first, into the world of high angst, in-your-face adolescence.

The hard-driver (high octane superwoman/man)

This third group is difficult to identify in children but is easy to spot in adults. Many first-borns are achievement-oriented individuals who drive themselves hard and often expect everyone else to work as hard as they do. These first-borns are high energy people who it seems just can't sit still. Not only do they want it all but they have to do it all. They don't make great team players, as they tend to leave other mere mortals in their wake. As leaders they need to slow down a little to let others catch up – slowing down is something that these people don't like to do.

If you are superwoman or superman you need to be efficient, driven, uncompromising, determined and able to operate at full-speed. You can pick these hard-drivers easily as during the week they work long, unrelenting hours and on the weekend they go home and run marathons or complete triathlons. Extreme sports were developed with this group in mind. Or they do garden makeovers or renovate their homes. This group is constantly on edge. As children these first-born hard-driver types are commonly diagnosed with Attention Deficit Hyperactivity Disorder (ADHD) and placed on Ritalin to calm them down. While some children undoubtedly have full-blown ADHD and need special assistance, too often high energy boisterousness is seen as more than what it is.

As the proportion of first-borns increases and more women perform the double shift of working and parenting I suspect this type of first-born female will become more common. These people need help unwinding. And indeed some never do. If you are married to a hard-driver type then you had better make sure you devote at least two weeks to any holiday as it will take this long for your partner to wind down, but make sure you book a place where there are plenty of activities. Even while relaxing they like to keep moving. These first-borns can be exhausting!

Dethronement

The outstanding fact about first-borns is that for a period they are single children – the star attraction in a new production for parents and grandparents. Suddenly, in at least 85 per cent of families, the first-born's world is shaken by the announcement of the arrival of another child on the scene. I say shaken because they are the sole objects of their parents' care for at least the first year of their life. It is an idyllic situation as there is no-one with whom they have to share their parents' time, energy or attention. They don't have to compete with anyone else for your attention, your care and your love. First-borns soon work out what it takes to get both their mother's and father's attention. The first-born cries and parents respond. Even if they choose not to respond it is generally a conscious choice. If first-borns could really ver-balise their thoughts when they are told for the first time that they are going to have a little brother or sister soon I am sure they would say: 'What? Is there going to be two of me soon?'

When the second child arrives the eldest doesn't see a playmate that you probably promised so faithfully. All the eldest generally sees is that you have brought home a pooing, weeing, crying machine that takes away mum and dad. While this may not be true from a parent's perspective it needs to be remembered that children don't gauge a situation objectively. They see things from their viewpoint and often their logic is faulty. When you look at the arrival of a second child through the eyes of a first-born it is not difficult to see that this interloper could well rob the first-born of mother's love. After all the newcomer is doing a good job of monopolising the parents, particularly the mother, in the early stages of life. The first-born cannot understand that their mother looked after them in exactly the same way and all this care she bestows on the newcomer doesn't mean that she loves the first-born any less. In many ways it is like approaching your partner and announcing that you have a new lover, who is moving in to live with you. Imagine asking your partner to help make your new lover feel welcome as they are going to be here to stay!

So first-borns feeling dethroned and losing their star of the family status try to recover their lost position or status in the family. They like to be in charge and often they will go to great lengths to impress upon their parents the second-born's short-comings. They will often be the first to let their parents know that the younger brother or sister is misbehaving – not so much to protect the younger one but to remind their parents of the inadequacies or poor behaviour of the interloper. From a first-born's perspective second-borns will always wear L-plates, or they would like to think they always will at any rate.

How to help first-borns cope with dethronement

When a new child arrives in a family, parents need to be aware of the first-born child's feelings of jealousy and displacement. The first-born cannot have all the attention and must realise that you need to spend time caring for the second-born, however the first-born needs to experience plenty of parental affection, care and attention. Make some time in your busy schedule to be alone with your first-born. Allow your first-born do something special that only big kids can do, whether it is sitting in a special chair or going to bed a little later. Let your first-born know in a tangible way that you realise that he or she is bigger and older than your second-born.

You may have to express your concerns to your relatives (grandparents, in particular), who can inadvertently pay the newcomer all the attention at the expense of the first-born. But they ignore the first-born usually at the parents' peril as the first-born will often act either in babyish ways (why not as it works for number two) or show off ('I guess I have to do something special or outrageous to be noticed') to gain the same amount of attention as the newcomer. The coming of the second-born demands tact on the part of parents and relatives, however if accomplished well there is every chance that the first-born will become a protective, friendly (but not always so) older sibling rather than being hostile and resentful.

Five strategies if you parent, work with, or live with a first-born

Taking life and themselves too seriously is the greatest problem facing many first-borns. They need to lighten up. However it must be said thank goodness for first-borns as without their drive, their leadership and their attention to detail nothing would ever get started let alone be completed. As they are such a prolific group in terms of sheer weight of numbers we all benefit when they learn to loosen up and enjoy themselves more. *Key message for most first-borns: loosen up.*

1. Encourage rather than criticise

As we have high expectations for first-borns there is a tendency to be critical of everything they do. First-borns respond better to encouragement than to criticism. Most parents know this but often have difficulty doing it with first-borns, as our expectations are so high.

First-borns respond better to encouragement than praise, but will settle for the latter if that is all they receive. Encouragement differs from praise in that it focuses on the process of what people do rather than the results of their activities. Encouraging language focuses on effort, improvement, contribution, and enjoyment and expresses confidence. You can always comment on a child's improvement, your workmate's efforts or your partner's assistance regardless of the results. Praise is saved for good results. First-borns need encouragement (but they often want praise) as it releases the pressure on them to perform. When they know that effort, improvement and contribution are more important to parents and teachers than good results they are more likely to take a few risks and stretch themselves.

2. Save some responsibilities for others

First-borns and functional first-borns know all about responsibility. Parents usually expect first-borns to look out for younger siblings at home and at school and they get more than their fair share of chores. Adolescent first-borns generally become experienced baby-sitters as parents often leave them in charge of younger brothers and sisters. First-borns are also reminded repeatedly to be good role models for their brothers and sisters. Many first-borns tell me that they resented the fact that they were always expected to behave well and set an example for their younger brother and sisters, who often behaved appallingly and were rarely rebuked.

Parents need to be careful not to heap all the jobs around the house onto the capable first-born's shoulders. This can be difficult as some eldest children thrive on responsibility but we need to save some jobs for younger children. Besides we need to allow responsible first-borns some time and opportunity to have some fun and put away their serious side.

3. Have special times and privileges

Recognise the special place of first-borns in the family by giving them some special privileges. Let them go to bed later than the others, have a special seat or be able to stay out a little later. They should experience some special privileges to balance the extra responsibility that they take.

4. Flaunt your imperfections

You may have guessed by now that many first-borns need loosening up so that they can lighten up, stretch themselves and take a few risks. As first-borns, more than children in any other position, take their behavioural cues from their parents it really helps if you can drop your guard and make a few mistakes. Wear a funny hat occasionally, drop a plate while emptying the dishwasher, let the sink overflow, forget to put petrol in the car, leave your clothes lying around the house or whatever it takes to show that you mess up too. Sometimes kids see adults as these big people who know it all and who never make mistakes! Just between you and me, they have this wrong!

5. Provide structure and rules

First-borns just love consistency. They love order and thrive on routines. They also need rules and limits. They may not always like them but they need them. Rules and routines put them in control as they feel safe and secure and they can predict your reactions. Some parents feel a little unsure about setting limits for kids but first-borns, in particular, need them. They will often take over or give parents a difficult time if they don't know where they stand or if parents feel a little unsure about setting rules.

Chapter 4

SINGLE CHILDREN – FIRST-BORNS WITHOUT SIBLINGS

The key to understanding only children is
to work out why they are only children.

Kevin Leman

Only children have an image problem. A concentrated public relations campaign is needed so that parents who have one child don't feel that they have to explain themselves to others and also children don't have to apologise for being the only pea in the pod. Perhaps the best way to change the image is to change the terminology we use. Many people who have one child don't do so by choice. They would like to have more but due to physical and other circumstances they have had to stop at one child. So rather than have an only child many parents I speak to have a single child in their family.

Only or single children have been the butt of more jokes and jibes than children in any other position. They are often portrayed as being selfish, unhappy, childish and attention-seeking. Alfred Adler, the father of birth-order theory, didn't have a high opinion of only children. He thought that they had dependency problems and had difficulties being contributing members of the groups they belong to as adults. Most of the recent research surrounding only children indicates that they are usually as well-adjusted as children in other positions. In fact, if self-esteem and school achievement levels are used as a barometer of a healthy, well-adjusted and desirable childhood then most parents would stop at one, as only children tend to perform admirably in these areas. The negative image of only children is a hangover from an era when big families were the norm, rather than the exception. Often children were single due to misfortune rather than by design. Frequently there was a mitigating factor such as divorce, family illness or a parental emotional problem that led to parents keeping their family to one child. Any problems or circumstances that existed within the family invariably impacted negatively on the child's personality development.

Interestingly, most parents who themselves were single children and who attend my birth-order seminars report that they either have more than one child or they want to have more than one. They recognise that while it may have been fine at the time not to be displaced by a sibling or compete for parental attention, they don't want a child of theirs to grow up as a single child in their families. It is almost as if they knew they missed out on something by being an only, but they are not sure what it is. It is ironic as they are the least equipped of children in any position to have a large brood. The lack of exposure to siblings as children means that such run-of-the-mill family issues as sibling fighting sometimes flummox single children when they are parents.

Single children by design, not by accident

In the 21st century the number of single children in families is increasing sharply, and currently 17.35 per cent of Australian families have just one child. Estimates indicate that this will increase to 20 per cent within a few years as more families decide that one child is sufficient. Quite simply, single children families are on the increase and are becoming an entrenched part of our social environment. Far from being a poorly regarded minority group single children have now joined the mainstream. More prolific than twins and more accepted than children with ADHD (those two other special interest groups), single children have arrived as a force. If single children were an Australian political party they would be challenging the 'major two' for supremacy.

Increasingly parents are making a lifestyle choice to stop at one child. Social research indicates that parents with one child are likely to be more educated, more liberal in their views, enter the relationship with their partner later and have their first child at a later date. With women bearing their first child at an increasingly older age the likelihood of having one child is far greater than ever. The reasons for the huge swing to parents having one child are complex. Financial pressures play a part. It has been estimated that raising two children until the age of 20 costs the average Australian family nearly $500,000. And this doesn't include the cost of a private education. The current propensity for Australians to crowd their lives with work and all sorts of activities makes parenting a large family particularly challenging. It is easier for parents to devote their meagre time and emotional resources to one child than to a whole brood. With many women and partners devoted to career or business-building at the peak childbearing age the physical and emotional resources of parents may be stretched indeed. Whatever the reason, one-child families are on the increase. If Alfred Adler was correct in his assumption 80 years ago that only children were more likely to grow up in a problematic family then he would have to rethink his views if he were around today. Single children today are more likely to be raised in a family that is financially secure, stable and content with their choice of one child.

What are single children really like?

Single children tend to be:
- achievement-oriented
- conservative
- confident
- articulate
- healthy in their self-esteem
- inflexible.

Single children are really first-borns who have never experienced the ignominy of dethronement. Their position in the family is assured. They share most of the characteristics of first-borns. In fact, Kevin Leman, author of *The New Birth Order Book*, refers to only children as 'super first-borns'. Many of the characteristics of first-borns, such as perfectionism, an achievement orientation and conservatism, are exaggerated in this group. Most research into birth order indicates that this group generally have healthy levels of self-esteem and are more confident and articulate than children in other situations. Certainly the fact that they spend a great deal of their early years in the company of parents who are not distracted by other children, and who can devote their considerable time, energy and parenting resources to just one child, gives them a huge academic advantage.

As they spend much of their early years in the company of adults only children are generally more articulate, confident and comfortable mixing with adults than children with siblings. Single children have two prime conditions in their favour. First, the ultra-stimulation that they gain from spending most of their early years in the company of adults gives a huge boost to their intellectual development. Conversations often revolve around adult interests and concepts, which can trigger their intellectual development far earlier than if they spent their entire early years surrounded by children. Also their tendency to spend more time alone means that they are more likely than other children to retreat to their very fertile imaginations. Their advanced verbal skills and interest levels can be a curse or a blessing. Sometimes single children are ostracised or teased by their peers, as they can seem a little aloof or different. On the other hand, some single children are so articulate and confident that it would take a brave child to tease them in the playground. A single child's temperament and upbringing is influential in determining how he or she interacts with peers.

Single children are usually perceived as self-centred and have difficulty sharing, however this is determined by how they are raised. If a parent places their single child on a pedestal, gives in to their every whim and limits their opportunity to mix with others the parent is teaching the child to think 'me' and not 'we'. On the other hand when a parent provides plenty of opportunities for single children to play with and spend time with friends from a young age they will invariably learn how to share their time, their space and more importantly their possessions with others.

All first-born children have a strong desire to please others, which is magnified in single children. These children only have their parents to measure and approve of their achievements when young so the need for recognition from elders is ever present.

Single children are frequently driven to achieve and succeed so they can please others rather than gain any innate satisfaction from a job well done. Single children who love to please always want adult approval. They drive parents mad with comments such as, 'How did I do, mum? Did I do well? Do you like what I have done?'

The desire for parental and adult approval can make them seem like perfect children. They often become like mini-adults, with perfect adult manners, and engage in activities whether at home or at school that gain high adult approval. An Australian single child is more likely to be found taking music lessons than making a mess in the backyard or playing in the street. He or she is more likely to be involved in activities that are supervised and structured by an adult than he is in activities that are unstructured, unsupervised and initiated by other children. The world of single children is usually ordered, safe and predictable.

You can rely on singles

As adults their reliability and conscientiousness ensure that these 'pleasers' are sensational assets to any organisation. Their ability to get things done combined with their attention to detail means that you can rely on these people, whether it is in completing a project, designing a blueprint or taking charge of customer service. You can leave them to work on their own and you can be assured whatever task they have been given will be completed well. However it is essential to give single children and adults due recognition for their achievements, as this is what drives them. Single children are more likely to follow directions than take the initiative so you may need to get them started on a task or project. But once they have begun a job you can rely on them to complete it. They are generally great project finishers but they have a tendency to sit back and act only when required.

Single children often share similar characteristics to the same-sex parent's birth position. Children strongly identify with their same-sex parents. They take many of their cues about how to view the world, how to relate to others and even how they should approach problems from the parent of the same gender. The power of modelling is indisputable but often over-looked. For instance, a girl whose mother was an easy-going, free-spirited youngest child might adopt a more relaxed attitude to life than if her mother was an achievement-oriented first-born. Similarly, a boy whose father is a conservative first-born would perhaps have a more serious, considered view of the world than he would if his father was a non-conforming second-born.

Singles can struggle to be kids

Single children frequently excel as mini-adults. I have known only-girls to hold lucid conversations with their mothers' friends and be the models of well-manicured young woman-hood. I have known only-boys to be well-mannered young men, confident and mature way beyond their years – perfect imitations of their fathers. Only children are frequently chil-dren that any parent would be proud of because they are so 'good' – and every parent wants 'good' kids. They are more likely to be clones of their parents than children in any other position and that means that more than children in any other position single children are more likely to be adult-like. The flipside is that only children have difficulty being childlike. They are often less playful and less 'silly' than children with siblings who have someone to be childlike with.

Single children tend to get very little input about how their world and their lives should be structured. The social environment for single children to some extent reflects their parents' ambitions and expectations of what a childhood should be. I suspect that everyone enters parenthood for the first time with some clearly defined views about the type of childhood they would like to provide. This view of childhood will be influenced by parents' early experiences as well as the ambitions and expectations they have for their young. I suspect that sometimes parents of single children believe that they have one shot at raising children and they are going to do it well. The loosening-up phenomenon and the change in perspective that occurs as parents have more children means that children generally have greater freedom to be masters of not only their own environments, but also inevitably their own destinies. The decision to engage in adult-initiated, supervised activities will more likely be made by children than adults the further down you are in the family tree. It is little wonder that youngest children are more likely than first-borns to take a few risks and are less concerned with parental approval than those first-borns and single children.

Handle with extreme care

Singles, whether adults or children, don't take well to criticism. They will take criticism personally, mistaking it for proof that they are just not good enough. Frequently they mistake constructive feedback for a personal attack. As a rule of thumb it is wise to give anyone praise or acknowledgment first before giving negative feedback, however it is critical to be constructive with this group. Singles can be resistant to change if they perceive that you are critical of them in any way, so it is best to swot up on the skill of encouragement if you work, raise or educate these children or adults.

Singles are used to life running fairly smoothly. They generally get the run of the kitchen, full access to their parents and they never have to wait in line for the bathroom or negotiate with a sibling to watch a television show. Life pretty much goes to plan for children when there are no siblings to contend with. Singles can be difficult to work and live with as adults because they expect life to continue to go to plan, just as it did as children. Flexibility or the Zen Buddhist notion of 'going with the flow' when events are out of their control do not come naturally to this group. They like order, routine and as few surprises as possible. It is not that this group is boring or lacks the ability to have fun. It is just that there is a time and a place for frivolity and fun – you need to pick the right time to be funny or frivolous if you work with or live with a single child.

Three types of single children

There are three common types of single children, as distinct from first-borns:
1. The assured individual
2. The ultra-perfectionist
3. The swinger.

The assured individual

Some single children are happiest working on their own or pursuing individual endeavours. It is not that they don't make good team members but rather group goals motivate them less than individual rewards. They often like the plaudits of their peers because they are accustomed to being the centre of attention. Confident and competent, these singles don't feel a huge need to compete with others for approval but they prefer to work and sometimes play on their own. As children they learned to occupy themselves and direct their own activities. Writing, art, graphic design, architecture and working from home are ideal for these assured individuals as they can work for long periods on their own and have little trouble disciplining themselves to complete their work. The assured individual doesn't suffer fools gladly and can be intolerant of those who are less talented than them.

These singles value their privacy and can be a closed book to their workmates and loved ones. As they are used to having their own way they find it difficult to compromise and see only one way to do anything – their way. As they have never been expected or taught to look after a sibling they can often have difficulty giving support to others.

The ultra-perfectionist

Many single children expect a great deal from the world as they are used to having their own way. They also expect the best and they usually get it. Some singles are charmers, skilled at manipulating those around them to get what they want or to achieve a goal. They value order and certainty and can become upset by mess, broken promises and inconsistency. Although they can sometimes fall short of achieving their full potential they often expect others to do their best.

This group have high expectations for themselves; however they will put off doing a job unless they can do it perfectly. In some ways this group often underachieve but they will always give the impression of being in control and on track. What other people see as minor problems these children can see as major disasters as they are used to everything going their way. This group can be extremely difficult to live and work with as they expect far too much of themselves and others.

The swinger

Some single children can be like two people trapped in the one body. They can be the height of sophistication one minute but throw a tantrum the next if they don't get their own way. They can be hooked on achievement one day and quite frivolous the next. Children with siblings soon learn that prima donna-type or erratic behaviour generally get them nowhere (or a thump behind the ear from an elder sibling) so they tend to cut out tantrums at some stage. As I have stated before, although the youngest in my family I was in many regards brought up as an only child due to the large gap between my siblings and myself. My prima donna single child tantrums used to work beautifully with my mother, as I only had to sulk for a few minutes for her to give me her full attention. Thankfully I had an older brother around to give me a reality check. Like many big brothers he had his own way of reminding me not to throw a tantrum or act like a crybaby, which was effective! My mother may have spoilt me but my elder brother was there to remind me what life was like in the real world inhabited by people roughly my own age.

The intensity factor

The factor that distinguishes single children is the intensity of the relationship they have with their parents. It is almost impossible for a mother's relationship with one child to be anything else but intense. With no other children to worry or think about the parental spotlight falls on just one child. This means that one child becomes the total focus of their parents' love, resources, energy and time. It is no wonder that single children do well academically, have healthy self-esteem and can feel self-assured and secure. The flipside of this total focus is that all the hopes and dreams that parents hold for their offspring fall on the shoulders of just one child. It can be quite a load for one person to carry. First-borns generally know all about their parents' hope and dreams – that's why expectations are high for first-borns. But the pressure eases a little with every subsequent child that comes into the family. Single children are the sole parental standard bearer. That's pressure! It is little wonder that Kevin Leman says that only children tend to be 'ultra-perfectionists'. They often put themselves down, make excuses for the slightest mistake and avoid tackling tasks where there is a risk of failure. The stakes are high for this group, as they don't want to disappoint their parents.

Parents of single children frequently lose their sense of proportion and little problems can seem like insurmountable issues. They frequently feel that they need to fix every problem or difficulty that their child has. When parents speak to me after a parenting seminar it is easy to pick those with one child. They tend to focus on the minute details of their child's life or worry about behaviours that parents of three or more children might not have even noticed. To give parents of only children a little perspective I often ask the question: 'Would you still worry about this issue if you had six children?' Invariably parents smile and admit that if they had six kids they would be far too busy to even notice the particular issue we are discussing. In large families children tend to look out for each other more than they do in small families. Even in my family of three, my eldest daughter frequently heard her younger sister read, helped her get ready for school and helped prepare her school lunch. These are all tasks that would probably fall on our shoulders if we only had one child.

In their terrific book *Birth Order and You*, Richardson and Richardson describe the intensity factor (p. 155). They warn that single children can become the sole focus of their parents' lives. Any emotional problems the parents have can be extremely harmful for only children who don't have peers to insulate them or provide a reality test. On a positive note Richardson and Richardson maintain that single children are likely to lead contented secure lives if their parents are emotionally comfortable themselves. It is apparent that single children often get a magnified dose of whatever their parents have – whether love, joy, anger or fear.

The challenge for all parents is to achieve the right balance between space and intimacy when raising their children. The notion of developing independence requires that we enable children to stand on their own two feet complete with their own ideas, views and values. We need to give children the space and opportunities to develop their own identities and to think for themselves. On the other hand we need to ensure that there are sufficient opportunities to develop healthy relationships with our children. There is no shortage of opportunities for parents to develop close relationships when they have one child, however many have difficulty allowing their child the space and freedom to become their own person.

Five strategies if you parent, work with, or live with a single

Like parenting any first-born it is important to get single children to loosen up and take themselves less seriously. More than children in any other position singles have difficulty just being children. Being the sole focus of the parental spotlight can have its drawbacks.

Key message for parents of singles: Give them space.

1. Be playful, silly and a risk taker yourself

Single children frequently live in an adult world and they don't have anyone to be childlike with at home. Fun and stupidity are helpful at home for single children so don't be afraid to put some music on, wear a funny hat, wrestle and play and just be plain stupid with your single child. This is a particular challenge if you are an only child or first-born yourself but it will do you good to loosen up. You will never replace a child as a live-in playmate but you can get across the notion that frivolity is fine and that your child should never be afraid to be childlike.

Make sure you provide your single child with as many opportunities to mix with those experts at play and frivolity – other children – from an early age. Also remember comments such as 'grow up' or 'I can't wait until you grow out of this silly stage you are in' are taboo in front of single children.

2. Don't over-indulge your child

It is helpful to make a concentrated effort not to spoil or over-indulge your single child. When we overprotect children or keep them from experiencing the usual scrapes of childhood we rob them of chances to handle problems. Similarly resist the temptation to give only children everything they want. Parents of singles are generally in a financially better position than parents with large families so it is within their reach to grant a child their every wish. The Rolling Stones had a message that all parents should listen to when they penned the song 'You can't always get what you want!' Often single children learn this lesson for the first time when they come to school, which can be quite a shock.

3. Don't see the child as a mirror of yourself

A challenge to all parents is to raise children so that they can be individuals able to stand on their own two feet, with their own ideas, values and lifestyle. When parents have more than one child their hopes and dreams tend to spread over a number of children. With a single child the hopes and dreams fall onto one set of shoulders.

4. Encourage your single child to mix with other children

Single children often don't have opportunities to share their space and time with others nor care for someone else in the family. Spending time with other children can help them develop the important social skill of sharing and also teach them how families with siblings operate. A seminar participant told me how an only child who stayed over for a sleepover at her place was so disturbed by the fighting and arguing between her two boys that he didn't return. This mother claimed that the arguing was nothing out of the ordinary but to the innocent eyes of a single child it was disturbing.

5. Make sure your single child keeps pets

Single children don't have the opportunity to care for others so keeping a pet is one practical opportunity for them to learn to look after something or someone other than themselves. Single children frequently have difficulties as parents as they haven't learned to care for anyone but themselves as children. Children need to have someone or something that relies on them so they can learn not only how to be reliable but develop the skills of nurturance.

Chapter 5

VICTIMS OF BAD TIMING – SECOND IN LINE OR STANDING IN THE MIDDLE

The second-born tries to live in harmony with the world.
Karl Konig

As families shrink in size there are fewer and fewer middles and increasingly more seconds. Second-born children have many characteristics in common with middle children. In fact, many seconds are also middle children so both these positions will be combined in this chapter. Many readers who were born second or who were the middle of more than three children would probably think: 'I have been sharing with someone all my life and I still have to share in a book about birth order. That's typical!'

Poor old second-borns. Get over it!

The middle (and in all likelihood the second) child is influenced by his or her elder sibling. A rule of thumb about birth order is that children are directly influenced by the sibling above and will differ from that sibling. Frank Sulloway, the author of *Born to Rebel*, puts it succinctly when he says that the first rule of the sibling road is that first- and second-borns will be different in personality, interests and achievement. Generally, the middle or second will be what the first-born isn't. He or she looks above and chooses interests and behaviours that are different to the elder sibling. If the first-born is responsible the next in line may well be a pest or at very least more relaxed. If the first-born is serious, as they often are, the second-borns may well be easy-going and gregarious. If the first-born is an academic star then there is a very good chance that the second will excel in another area such as the arts or on the sports track. Sometimes the differences are extremely subtle. Australian cricketing twins Steve and Mark Waugh both excel in the same field of endeavour however they both play cricket with fundamentally different styles reflecting their birth-order characteristics. Steve, the functional eldest (his brother is often referred to as 'Junior'), plays like a first-born. He is a hard-driving leader with immense powers of concentration. He is goal-oriented as he is renowned for keeping one eye on his batting average, which hovers around the magical 50 runs per innings mark. His brother Mark plays the game with all the flair and panache of the free-spirited second-born that he is. He has often been criticised for his apparent lack of application when at the batting crease or for giving away his wicket too easily. His average is considerably lower than his brother's and his general demeanour is different. Nonchalance, flair and grace are hallmarks of Mark's cricketing style unlike his brother who has cut out most of the risky shots from his batting repertoire.

Sometimes the second-born is able to compete in the same area filled by the first-born. If he or she competes successfully there is every chance that they will reverse roles. For instance, if the second of two boys is physically stronger, more athletic or blessed with extra intelligence than the elder sibling then he may become more dominant, while the elder slips back into second place. Alternatively if a second-born girl is born with a temperament or physical attributes that are favoured by her parents, in particular, her mother, then she may gain more of the privileges and plaudits that are normally reserved for the first-born. If a first-born has an illness or a condition such as Attention Deficit Hyperactivity Disorder (ADHD) then the second-born will gain more favourable attention while the eldest may be given very little responsibility or opportunities to be the 'eldest'. Birth order has more to do with how a person functions than merely the position that they take in the family.

The arrival of the second-born is different

The birth of the first-born may be a life-changing event for parents however the arrival of the second doesn't draw the same amount of attention. It is not so much that parents have 'been there and done that' but their life has already been altered and a pattern of life has emerged that includes another entity. One more mouth to feed and set of nappies to change isn't going to alter your life too much. It has been dramatically changed already.

The preparation for the birth of the second child isn't so focused or intense as it was for the previous birth. Many parents use a name left over from the first-born child. They don't attend as many antenatal classes, if at all. They are generally too busy with the first-born child to get away. Preparations for the second-born often include moving the first-born from a basinet to a cot or from one room to another to make room for the new arrival. The impending birth of the second generally brings with it a period of disruption for the first-born. Wise parents also devote a significant amount of time before the birth preparing the first-born for the impending event.

The arrival of the second may not be a life-changing event for parents however it is a life-changing event for the first-born. When you look lovingly down at the second-born as you hold it in your arms you instinctively know that you will be sharing this child, as well as your time and energy, with the first-born. While the first-born got all of you without interruptions, number two is going to share you with another. If the first-born is an experiment and groundbreaker, the second-born is a rival to the first-born for your attention, energy and approval. Second-borns often try to keep up with the first-born so they often crawl and walk at an earlier age. This pattern follows throughout childhood as seconds are often introduced to leisure activities, clubs and sporting activities at an earlier age than their sibling. This is natural, as they tend to tag along with number one and follow in the groundbreaker's footsteps. The first-born has a vested interest in keeping the second child in his or her place, or at least being seen to be superior or better. He or she will often go to great lengths to remind their parents of their superiority. First-borns often point out their second sibling's misbehaviours or inadequacies to their parents just in case they haven't noticed. Number ones often don't leave such matters to chance. So the second faced with competition will go either head to head or develop their own unique personality, traits and characteristics. They often excel in areas that are left-over by the first-born.

The second-born child leads a different life to that of the first-born. His or her life will in all likelihood revolve around the life of the first-born. Seconds had better get used to tagging along after the first-born because they will in all likelihood accompany the first-born to playgroup and preschool activities. They are often woken from their afternoon naps so adults can pick up the first-born from school. Second-borns learn to fit in so flexibility is often a key component of their personality.

It's not fair!

Second and middle children are generally the victims of poor timing. They were born too late to get the perks of their eldest siblings and, if they have younger siblings, too early to benefit from the more relaxed style of parenting that they generally experience. They also tend to get more hand-me-downs, spend less time on their own with their parents and have to fit their life around the eldest who is the first to establish a life pattern. Seconds who are middle children are something of a paradox. It is important to look closely at those children above and below them to understand a particular middle child. In particular, the distribution of ages is crucial in understanding the development of a middle child's interests and birth-order personality. Middle children tend to develop birth characteristics in relation to the children they are closest to in age or spent more time with when they were young. The following examples show how the middle child can develop in different ways according to the constellation of ages and genders that surround them.

Hypothetical development of middle children

Family A	Family B
Female – 15	Male – 14
Female – 13	Female – 9
Male – 8	Female – 7
Male – 6	Female – 6

The second child in Family A is closest in age to the first-born so in all likelihood she will develop the characteristics of a second-born. She will more than likely develop a set of personality traits and interests quite diverse from her older sibling, who is of the same gender. On the other hand, the second-born in Family B may be like a first-born as she is closer in age to her younger sisters than to the first-born. The third-born child in this family will in all likelihood develop second-born or middle child tendencies as she is the second of three girls born very close together. I would suspect that the seven year old in Family B would be in the least favoured position being squeezed above and below by siblings of the same gender. Generally if all siblings are the same gender, the child in the middle is at the greatest disadvantage. They generally receive less parental attention than their siblings so often they find their own less savoury ways to gain some parental attention. They can be the proverbial 'black sheep' of the family, dropping out from family-favoured activities, occupations or lifestyle choices. If the rest of the family are career-oriented a middle girl may be a homemaker, if the others are academic then the middle girl may choose non-academic activities in which to excel. Middle children of the same gender generally choose a different path than their siblings.

Life is usually better for middle siblings if they have siblings of a different gender. They can be 'special' (which every child secretly craves) and receive plenty of parental attention due to their gender. Its seems that most parents want at least one child of each gender so these middle children can be in a favourable position. If they are surrounded by girls, middle boys can sometimes have difficulty making friends with other boys but they often have little trouble forming relationships with girls, particularly if they were close to their sisters. A boy in this position probably needs to have a close relationship with his father so that he can establish his gender identity. When it comes to middle children a child who is a different gender to the first but the same as the last is in the most favourable position. They probably don't experience the same amount of pressure as their eldest sibling although the expectations on their shoulders would still be a factor to consider. However they are the first of their gender and experience some of the privileges and even adulation of this position. There is every chance that the middle will be asked to look out for their younger sibling and often have the younger sibling around for many of their childhood activities.

What are seconds really like?

Second-born children often become the free spirit of the family or the child most likely to upset (annoy, hassle) siblings. If you have three children sitting quietly watching television and you suddenly hear a yelp coming from the television room you can bet that the middle child has disturbed the peace in some way. Perhaps the middle child has thumped the youngest or flicked the eldest with a ruler or some foreign object. Middles can be like that! They like to get even!

Characteristics of second and middle children

Seconds and middles tend to be:
- flexible
- diplomatic
- peacemakers
- free spirits
- generous
- competitive.

Seconds who are also middles classically make great 'people' people and are often the most resilient of adults. They are the hardest to pin down as their personality is influenced by those around them, particularly their eldest sibling and the constellation of their family. Many seconds are rebellious, more likely to act in outrageous or unpredictable ways. During a birth-order workshop I conducted for an industry organisation I asked the participants to place themselves into groups according to their birth position. I then placed a sheet of paper in front of them and stood back and observed what happened. The sheet gave instructions for a group activity. Not surprisingly the eldest-borns were the first to begin. They sat in a tight-knit group and went about their task diligently. The singles were next to begin and the youngest-borns typically didn't make a start until I prompted them. They had a great chat though. The representative of the seconds who picked up the instruction sheet did something that is typical of many second-borns – when she read the task she ripped the paper to shreds indicating that she wasn't going to be part of my activity. Seconds can be contrary. They can also be sociable. This organisation had a friendly relaxed feel to it, which was surprising given that its industry typically attracted a large proportion of first-borns. However this activity showed that a high of percentage of employees were second-borns. No wonder the organisation enjoyed such a friendly atmosphere!

If I were going to place anyone on the front desk of an organisation or require a negotiator with a flexible set of communication skills I would go for a second-born every time. As children they couldn't use power or charm to get their own way with eldest children so they learned to negotiate and compromise instead. These children learn the hard way that human relationships are about give and take, compromise and even missing out occasionally.

Second children learn early in life to be flexible as they are generally expected to fit into the life of the first-born. From the start their lives are organised around the life of the first-born child. This is less so if both children spend their early years in child care but if children are cared for at home then the second is more likely to have feeding times, play periods and sleeps organised around the routine of the first-borns. Such is the life of the second. In many ways second-borns expect less from life than first-borns and only children and are less upset by change and adversity than their first-born counterparts. Kevin Leman in *The New Birth Order Book* claims that middle children are generally more independent and mentally tougher than any other birth position. While this is a positive characteristic he also claims that second-borns are the people least likely to reach out for help when they need it. Middles often learned to keep to themselves and get by on their own resources as kids. They are also renowned for being secretive, confiding in friends more than family members, both their joys and problems. They learn early in life to play their cards close to their chests as they can get burned when insensitive siblings have access to their inner thoughts.

Looking outside the family for belonging

Middle children usually have larger friendship groups than their elder siblings. Being surrounded by siblings may lead them to be more gregarious however there is a deeper reason for their propensity to make friends. Seconds learn early that they can't always hang with an elder sibling and if they have younger siblings then they can't always run to parents for help. Seconds turn naturally to their peers as allies. They will often seek membership of other groups such as sports teams, clubs or even gangs in an effort to belong on their own merits. Seconds want to experience a group as their own free from sibling interference and parental control. They are also generally the first children to leave the family home. Or they may as an adult move to another state or city. It is not that they are trying to escape their family or that the family ties are not strong. Rather their need for family acceptance and recognition is not paramount. They can seek their sense of belonging elsewhere.

Three types of second-borns

Although a difficult group to pinpoint there are three broad types of second-borns:
1. The socialiser
2. The justice seeker
3. The diplomat.

The socialiser

Sit back at the next function you attend and observe those people who are adept at moving easily from group to group. My guess is that it will be second-borns who work the room best. At work watch those who will respond readily to the interruptions of a workmate and engage in a conversation while those around are beavering away. There is a good chance it is second-borns who love to have a chat at work. Next time you fill up the car with petrol or you visit a supermarket notice if the person behind the counter strikes up a friendly conversation with you. My hunch is that it will be a second-born who tries to strike up a conversation behind the counter. Many seconds by their nature make great socialisers.

Even second-borns who are in leadership positions bring their social skills and propensity to mix with others to the job. In fact they often make charismatic leaders, adept at mixing with others and putting them at ease. It is no coincidence that Australia's leading prime ministerial candidate of recent years as 'man of the people', Bob Hawke, was a second-born. Hawke was widely recognised for the ease with which he was able to mix with people of all walks of life. He was known as a great socialiser. These types of leaders are not renowned for their organisational abilities so they need people around them who can handle the fine details.

Second-born children are usually more sociable than their elder siblings, spending more time in the company of their peers. In fact, many seconds just can't stand being left out of any social activity even preferring to go to school with an illness rather than miss a fun event or activity. All this social activity is great training for later life and it is little wonder that second-borns are an asset to any team as they can be the social glue that holds a group together.

The justice-seeker

Seconds and middles, in particular, often develop an acute sense of justice. As children they often experience life as being unfair to them compared to their siblings, particularly those who are squeezed between siblings of the same · gender. Resilient seconds don't spend too much time fretting over the fact that the eldest gets more privileges while the youngest sibling is spoilt rotten. They learn that making a fuss gets them nowhere so they get on with life. However they can dig their heels in over a cause or an issue that first-borns see as trivial and youngest-borns don't even notice. They can appear stubborn as they refuse to budge on an issue such as television viewing – they may give ground on most things but seconds will often draw the line on some issues – after all 'it is only fair that I have my way sometimes'.

Second-borns are frequently labelled rebellious. Indeed they often rebel against orthodox thinking, refusing to act in ways that parents approve of or even failing to toe the company line at work. One second-born who worked in a tier-one law firm wore the regulation suit and tie to work as was company practice but was known for wearing bright red cowboy boots. It was an odd combination but it was an effective form of protest that sent the message, 'I play your game of dress-ups but I think it is a silly one.' Alfred Adler said of second-born children, 'he is inclined to believe . . . that there is no power in the world which cannot be overthrown'.

On a broader scale I have found that many second-borns have a strong sense of social justice and are likely to get behind a cause particularly if it involves protecting someone who is the victim of some type of political or social injustice. Seconds can be drawn to helping professions such as medicine, psychology, and social work or volunteer their time to organisations such as Amnesty International and Australian Volunteers Abroad as they have a highly developed sense of justice. They genuinely want to right some of the wrongs of the world or help those on the wrong end of injustice. While firsts often need a purpose in their lives if they are to feel successful, many seconds need to get behind a cause to give their lives meaning.

The diplomat

'Blessed are the peacemakers.' Middle children may learn early that it is easier to keep the peace with siblings on either side than get involved in an endless round of conflict. Compromise is something that they are adept at as they learned that it is usually easier to give in to their siblings' wishes than fight over every issue. The advantage of being surrounded by siblings is that you can vacillate between the two or two groups when it suits. Middles often learn how to play with older children but if an older sibling is not around they often play with a younger sibling. They learn to adapt not only to different personalities but also to the needs and norms of different age groups. They first experience a sibling's move into adolescence and the changes that this means can be confounding. 'Why can't I go into the bathroom any more?' 'Why is she so mean all of a sudden?' Why doesn't he want to play with me like he used to?

Second-borns frequently learn to get along with adolescent family members before their parents.

Seconds are often better at seeing issues from different sides. First-borns often see the world through one lens – their own. Seconds and middles learn to see different points of view and are generally more empathetic than any other birth position.

Five strategies for raising seconds or middles

In this current era of small families second-borns can function like first-borns as they may be the first of their gender. However second-borns generally have more behaviour problems at home and at school than children in any other position. They often feel squeezed or that life is unfair.

Key message for raising or teaching second-borns: help them feel special.

1. Never compare a second-born to a sibling

Statements such as 'Your elder sister was a star. Why can't you be more like her?' that are often muttered out of frustration only demotivate middle and younger siblings. Sibling comparison shows a lack of understanding of the effects of birth-order on a child's personality development. The second or middle looks above and if he or she sees a sibling who is smarter, faster or more capable then there is every chance that he or she will choose a different path to excellence.

Sometimes comparison can be so subtle that we don't recognise it. One mother placed a graduation photograph of her eldest child in pride of place at home. She didn't realise that this was a source of discouragement for her second child who was struggling at school. In the words of the second-born: 'That photo of

Sophie was placed above the dining table for everyone to see. It was a reminder of what success meant to my parents. As I ate breakfast every morning I was reminded by that photo what my parents expected of me and I knew that I could never be successful like her. So I didn't try at school any more. It was easier being difficult than trying to live up to their expectations.'

2. Help them find their own area of expertise

The best way to help second children achieve is to help them find their own area of expertise that may be different from those that parents and teachers value. They need their own exclusive patch of turf where they can shine. This is difficult when children are young but as they move through childhood and into adolescence many opportunities open up to them at school and within the community where they can excel. It is essential that you value their areas of interest, even if they differ from your own. If your child stakes a claim to fame in music or sport rather than academic success, which you may value highly, then it is important that you accept and take a personal interest in his or her area of expertise.

3. Listen to this child

Seconds are often ignored or act up to be heard so they will respond to adults who are willing to listen to and take an interest in them. Seconds can be secretive and keep their opinions to themselves so tread carefully and take the time to listen to seconds when they have something to say. Their voice often becomes lost in the crowd at home or they learn that the eldest takes up more of their parents' time and energy.

4. Initiate one-on-one time with your second-born

In a three-child family second-borns tend to spend less one-on-one time with their parents than the other two children. First-borns have had their parents to themselves for the first period of their lives and youngest-borns tend to spend more time in the company of parents when the older children have gone to school or moved onto different interests in adolescence. You may have to initiate some time with your child by inviting them along when you go shopping, watching some sporting activity together or even taking them on an outing on their own. Sharing an interest or activity is one tangible way of forging a strong relationship with your second child

5. Don't let them avoid conflict

While some middle children may be our future diplomats others will do anything to avoid confrontation. They need to learn that compromise means finding common ground rather than just giving in when they meet with either power or influence exerted by another person. These children can close up to avoid conflict or making waves. You may have to challenge second-born girls, in particular, to stick up for themselves rather than give in to avoid an argument.

Chapter 6

MASTERS OF CHARM – YOUNGEST CHILDREN

The youngest may have been born last but he has a sixth sense that tells him that he is not going to be least.

Kevin Leman

The world would be a boring, straight place if it were not for later-borns. In fact, if not for later-borns we would still be living in caves, as it is this birth-order personality that is most likely to think: 'There must be another way of doing this!' Youngest-borns are often more creative, more innovative and, as Frank Sulloway found in his extensive birth-order research, most likely to challenge conventional thinking and propose radical ideas. That is quite a wrap and one that most youngest-borns would feel uncomfortable with, as they usually don't take themselves so seriously. After all they have learned that few others take them seriously enough for their liking.

Youngest children are born into a position that is quite different to their siblings, particularly if their families are small.

They are in the fortunate position of having a sibling break their parents in for them and they don't have the pressures of the first-born. Their birth is not the big event like the first-born's arrival. Some parents are still thinking of a name when they are putting the birth notice for the youngest in the paper! 'Ah what will we call him? Jarred will do. Yeah, that sounds fine.'

Youngest children are indebted to their siblings for breaking their parents in for them. It was a sibling who introduced their parents to each stage of development providing those first experiential lessons about infancy, toddlerhood, preschool, primary school and adolescence. It was a sibling who experienced all the parental anxiety and ineptitude that comes with being new to the job of child rearing. Parents are more relaxed about the whole child rearing process by the time the youngest comes along unless there have been unfortunate circumstances such as a long-term illness or even the death of a sibling, which fuels parental anxiety. Greater parental experience usually brings a greater perspective and heightened sense of what is really important. More experienced parents are less likely to fuss over a child's every sniffle or worry about getting everything right. Parents are obsessive and have strong ideas about most things pertaining to first-borns. I was adamant that my eldest child wouldn't watch an M-rated movie in my home until he was the recommended age of 15. We had many arguments about what was suitable viewing for him when he was in those difficult in-between years of 13 and 14. In stark contrast my youngest child had seen many of those movies by the time she had turned 14. It was not so much that my parenting standards had slipped. It was more that I was realistic about the types of movies she could cope with and was aware that the inflexible 'thou shalt not' type of attitude was not helpful in the least.

Parents are harder to impress

If parents are more relaxed about their child rearing by the time the last-born comes along then the youngest generally finds that they have to work harder to impress parents with their knowledge, skills and new-found abilities. It is hard to get over-awed with a child's success at potty training, a toddler's building efforts or a preschooler's work of art when it is your third or fourth time around. You have seen it all before. It is not that parents aren't pleased about children's accomplishments but it is like hearing a joke for the umpteenth time – you may laugh to be polite but it is hard to feel genuine excitement. Parents also tend to be a little impatient with the youngest child's development. 'Did it really take this long for the others to walk, talk and read?'

Parental expectations tend to be far less for youngest-borns who experience less pressure to achieve than first-borns. As the following letter shows parental expectations can have a huge bearing on a child's self-perception:

> I am the youngest of three girls with a six-year age difference top to bottom. Both my older sisters were very academically bright. So was I but I never appreciated it. My parents never pressured me to do overly well at school so that they didn't force me to compete with my sisters' high standards. Inadvertently they sent me the message that I wasn't as capable as my older siblings. So I felt that I wasn't as good as them and that perhaps I was a disappointment. Being the third girl I was aware at a subtle level that 'I should have been a boy', so even though not a word was ever spoken, my gender and birth order had an impact on my own self perceptions – real or otherwise! (Juliet Dougherty)

Some parents take their teaching and training duties less seriously with the youngest child. There are a couple of possible reasons for this. For a start they have to share their time between more children and they have only so much time and energy to share. Parents often experience 'teaching fatigue' by the time the last-born comes along. Often older siblings take a significant role in training and teaching younger children, which helps to promote their independence but in some ways reinforces the youngest child's position of dependence on others. In my own family, my eldest daughter spent countless hours reading storybooks and novels to her younger sister as they were tucked up in bed at night. The younger one was content to have someone read for her so she took a long time before reading at night became a habit.

One of the traits many last-borns share is persistence. They learn when they are young that if they persist with what they want they will outlast their siblings and wear their parents down eventually. Youngest children in the family are typically charmers and manipulators. They love to get their own way – and they invariably do. Youngest children are born into the unenviable position where everyone in the family is bigger, brighter and more capable than them. They are surrounded by people who can read better, who are smarter and who can even tie shoelaces up in a flash while they struggle.

They also have difficulty being taken seriously by others. And it seems everyone likes to remind them of their incapabilities, particularly the eldest child in the family. 'You're too small to be able to do that' is a sentence many youngests are familiar with. A wise youngest will never compete against the first-born unless he or she knows what is good for them. They learn not to try to outrun or outsmart their eldest sibling – it is unwritten law in most families that the youngest child should know his or her place. However youngest children learn that they can usually outlast an eldest child if they really want something, so persistent nagging, complaining or other annoying behaviours are things that really pay off for youngest children.

Charm and cuteness also have huge pay-offs for children in this position. Youngest girls usually have their fathers wrapped around their little fingers. They soon learn that they only have to look cute or vulnerable or feign incompetence and a male adult will come to their aid. Youngest boys often have a similar effect on mothers who are known to refer to their sons as the 'baby of the family' even when they may be fat, balding and forty. If parents' pride is the first-born then their joy is often found in the youngest child.

Turning dependence into an artform

If there is one skill that youngest children learn to perfect it is the ability to place other people in their service. What is the point of being surrounded by capable people if you can't exploit the situation or, at least, turn it to your advantage? Watch a youngest child mix with others. They can have others doing all sorts of mundane things for them that eldest children wouldn't dream of outsourcing. For instance, my youngest child for years has sat back and subtly had her siblings running all sorts of errands for her. If she is watching television and wants a drink of water she will wait until another family member goes into the kitchen and then very politely ask them to bring her a drink. A simple request for assistance with homework will often result in a parent doing the whole task for her. As with most youngest children her ability to outsource tasks is subtle but effective.

Recently, a woman approached me after a seminar where I spoke about the propensity for youngest-born to place others in their service. She told me how the youngest of her four boys, who quite dutifully assumed the role of the baby of the family, continued as an adult to turn to others to help him out of any difficult situation. Once when his car broke down the 28-year-old family baby rang his mother and asked if she could pick him up. When I asked this mother how she responded she just looked at me incredulously and replied: 'Why, I picked him up of course!' Youngest-borns have that effect on people!

Youngest children often experience less discipline than other siblings. Richardson and Richardson in their book *Birth Order and You* suggest that youngest children frequently believe that rules are meant for other people, rather than them. In many cases parents are far less strict on youngest children than they were on the elder children. As the youngest child in my own family I experienced far greater freedom than my siblings and greater leniency from my parents if I broke a rule. I sensed they were tired by the time I came along and would only engage in battles with me over really important issues – they ignored trivial misdemeanours such as messy bedrooms or coming home late, which had resulted in being grounded for my elder siblings. I know I had it easy compared to my siblings!

What are youngest children really like?

Kevin Leman in *The New Birth Order Book* describes youngest children as 'ambivalent'. I have heard youngest children described as many things – charmers, spoilt, dependent, manipulative, affectionate, are common descriptors – but ambivalence is new, although it makes sense. Many youngest-borns have two faces or two sides to them that are opposite to each other. They can be extremely happy or extremely sad, they can be clowns one minute, making everyone laugh, but the next minute they wear a frown as if they carry the worries of the world. They can be affectionate and withdrawn in one day. They can be easy-going most of the time and then they can snap and be the most difficult people to deal with for no apparent reason. There is often no middle ground with many youngest children – their emotional world is often black or white, rarely grey. Leman offers no reason for this ambivalence apart from attributing it to the fact that they often experience extremes of parenting, ranging from nurture one minute to being poked fun at or taken lightly the next.

Characteristics of youngest children

Youngest children are often:
- risk-takers
- persistent
- outgoing
- charmers
- ideas people
- creative
- challenge authority.

'Notice me!' is the way some young children seem to act. Youngest children can be quite paradoxical. They are less concerned about gaining parental approval than first-borns yet they crave attention. They are suckers for praise and encouragement. Unlike their eldest siblings, youngest-borns enjoy praise and encouragement for the attention rather than the approval. Perhaps all those years of not being noticed or listened to or taken seriously, have taken their toll. Nothing they do is very big news as someone else has generally done it before. They are not the first to walk, talk, tie shoelaces or begin school. Perhaps that's why the performing arts, such as acting and comedy, hold such an attraction for youngest-borns. Many youngest children learned that entertaining and making their peers and siblings laugh are great ways to gain some recognition. They use their cuteness to great effect – getting laughs but without offending others.

Youngest children are more likely to be divergent thinkers and find their own way of doing things. As they are less concerned with gaining parental approval than first-borns youngest-borns are less bound by parental constraints. Freed from the burden of wanting to please their parents and not experiencing the pressure of high expectations youngest-born children tend to find their own path and achieve in areas that are unusual for their family. It is perhaps for these reasons that creative, artistic pursuits are full of later or last-borns, whereas first-borns are more likely to end up in positions of leadership.

Last-born boys tend to be more impetuous than children in any other position – they act now and worry about the repercussions later. Their impetuosity can be a worry for parents as their tendency to jump first and think later can be downright dangerous. Youngest children learn that they can throw caution to the wind if there is a supportive, responsible elder sibling around to look after and protect them. Why worry when there is someone else to do the worrying for you?

The positive aspect is that youngest children are more likely to stretch themselves into new areas of endeavour and try new experiences than their elder siblings. If youngest-born children are successful they will tend to be successful on their own terms, rather than try to compete with an older sibling. So if older siblings are successful in school and have high status jobs don't be surprised if the youngest sibling just scrapes through school but excels in sport, the arts or another area of interest. As adults youngest-born children often don't take career success as seriously as first-borns. Work satisfaction, friendships and personal well-being often rank higher than career advancement for youngest-borns. It is little wonder that youngest-borns tend to be followers rather than leaders.

Last-borns can appear a little self-centred, which is probably due to the fact that they tend to do less at home to help others. Parents often forget to give chores and other household responsibilities to the last-born. But even if they give them responsibility some youngest-born children will drag the chain allowing older siblings to do most of their jobs. Youngest-born children can stay babies for a long time!

Three types of youngest children

There are three broad types of youngest children:
1. The impatient doer
2. The ideas person
3. The salesperson.

The impatient doer

Ever been on a committee where you have discussed a serious matter and the opinions have flown thick and fast? Everyone is involved in the discussion except for one person who sits fidgeting and wearing a 'get on with it' type of expression. The chances are that it is a youngest sitting there bored with the discussion. Many youngests are the personification of the old Nike slogan – 'Just do it'. As children they may like to think now and worry about the consequences later and as adults they like to jump into new projects feet and all, often without weighing up the pros and cons. Youngest-borns can be a fantastic asset to any group as they are often the initiators of activities – the first up on the dance floor or the first to try a new idea at work. They may need others around them to temper their impetuosity and remind them that the risks of failure have dire consequences.

The ideas person

If you are stuck for creative ideas then look for a youngest to inspire you. They may not get hands-on and solve your problems but they just may work out how it should be done. Artistic and creative challenges are made for the divergent thinking of youngest-borns. This cohort tends to be free from conventional thinking and is not afraid to try something new or different. Many youngest-borns appear to be absent-minded, even vague, but don't be fooled. They can be sharp as a tack when you put them in the right environment or give them an opportunity to think of some ideas or use their creative flair.

The salesperson

The birth-order personality of many youngest-borns has three attributes that make them fantastic salespeople, whether in a professional sense or just in the sense of selling ideas. First, they are tenacious and learn not to take 'no' for an answer. A true youngest knows that there is a way around everything and that objections simply mean that you have to try harder to make another person say 'yes'. Youngest-borns often learn as children that if their mother says 'no' to a request she will eventually change her mind if they keep at her. Last-borns have a way of wearing down even the strongest resistance and getting their own way. Second and youngest children relate well to other people – they are people-oriented. They may talk too much and for too long but they are generally likeable people, which is a huge asset in any area of sales. Third, youngest-borns like to play and have fun. Their propensity for fun can be disarming. Some years ago I was looking at some cars in a car yard. My defences went up as a salesman approached. With a broad grin he said, 'Go ahead. Take a look around. If you see anything you like just let me know and you can take it for a ride. Just have some fun.' His friendly attitude won me over completely. I didn't buy one car from him; I bought two – one for my wife, Sue, and one for myself. As I signed the papers I asked him about his position in his family, suggesting that he probably was the youngest. He looked at me in dismay and revealed that he was the youngest of six children and the only boy. No wonder he liked to have fun!

With their propensity for fun and playfulness, their persistence and their excellent people skills, it is little wonder that last-borns make great salespeople.

Five strategies for raising youngest-borns

Youngest-borns are reminded every day that there is someone bigger, smarter and more capable than them so they often act out the helpless role that others can thrust upon them. They are also adept at putting others to work for them.

Key message for raising or teaching youngest-borns: let them take responsibility.

1. Don't let them get lost

Youngest children can easily get lost in the crowd. Their accomplishments don't seem to be such the big deal as they were for elder siblings. Make a fuss out of their accomplishments. The art they bring home may be the fourth finger-painting you have received but it is your child's first, so be surprised.

They can sometimes be teased, put down or laughed at by siblings and you don't even know it. So it helps to give these kids some ideas to help them stand up for themselves. I remember giving my youngest daughter some practical assertiveness lessons to help her combat some teasing from her older brother. He would call her names and she would either come to me or scream at him in a high-pitched voice, which was exactly the type of reaction that he was hoping for. She practised standing in a strong manner and rehearsed some lines such as, 'Thank you very much for your opinion but I happen to think otherwise.' Such lines were designed to take the wind from his sails and let him know that she wasn't going to get involved in his games.

This group are used to sitting back so make sure their voice is legitimately heard. Sometimes older siblings do most of the talking for the youngest child. A stranger may ask your youngest his or her name and an elder sibling may well tell them. Youngest children often get used to sitting back and allowing elder siblings to do all the talking at family gatherings or share news with relatives. You may need to be proactive yourself and invite your youngest to tell grandma about the family holiday or order the fish 'n' chips at the takeaway.

2. Give them responsibilities

Youngest-borns sometimes get the message that nothing they do is good enough so they become masters at ducking work or being helpless. Don't be fooled. Make sure these children have plenty of opportunities to help so they feel important. It is easy to fall into the trap of giving all the responsibilities to the children who are already capable rather than to the children who need to develop this characteristic.

My children's ability to cook decreases as we move down the family. First-born Sam was given plenty of cooking lessons and opportunities to cook so that by the time he was finished primary school he was cooking a family meal once a week. Fast-forward to youngest Sarah and I was shocked by how little cooking knowledge she had by the time she finished primary school. It was not so much lack of interest but lack of opportunity as by then her elder siblings were adept in the kitchen so she took the youngest route – feigned ineptitude – and I fell for it. One way to do a child a disservice is to spoil, pamper or expect very little of them. Their self-confidence plummets and they become locked in a cycle of low self-esteem. It is youngest children who are most likely to be pampered, protected or kept the family baby. Keep a roster of jobs and make sure that the youngest gets his or her fair share of family responsibilities.

3. Encourage them to make their own decisions

Youngest-borns are used to following the crowd and become expert at avoiding decision-making about a whole range of things. Let them choose from menus, decide what you (or they) should cook for dinner, what they should wear and what movie the family should watch.

4. Put pressure on them

If we need to loosen up on first-borns we often need to put considerable pressure on youngest children to put their head down and produce decent work at school. Sometimes being the youngest allows them the luxury of getting away with poor work efforts. Don't be surprised if you find yourself continually reminding the youngest-borns to apply his or herself a little harder. This group is skilled at getting away with being less than well-behaved so make sure they experience the consequences of their actions. As most researchers seem to agree that youngest children are less likely to experience discipline and most likely to get a favoured run from parents, it is useful to make a list of some of the rules, responsibilities and privileges involving children at different ages. This will help you make life a little more equitable for your youngest.

5. Let go – resist the temptation to hold on

There is a tremendous temptation for parents to keep their youngest babies for longer than other children. We generally can't wait for the first-born to grow up however we often resist the youngest's efforts to grow up because growing up means growing away at some point. When my first-born told me he didn't need me to walk him to class in the morning I felt happy as this was a sign that he was growing up. I welcomed his maturity. When my youngest proudly announced that she was too old to walk to the classroom with her father I felt sad, as this was another sign that my youngest was growing up and away from me.

Chapter 7

HOW GENDER
AFFECTS BIRTH-ORDER
PERSONALITY

*For many boys, one of the great sins
of the age is to be different.*

Dr Tim Hawkes

Gender impacts on a child's personality development for both sociological and biological reasons. While girls and boys have many biological characteristics in common there are many fundamental physiological differences between the genders. These biological differences impact on a child's birth-order personality, but more importantly it is the socialisation factors that have the greatest impact on gender differences. In the 1970s and 1980s when I was teaching it seemed that teachers and, to a lesser degree, parents forgot to treat the genders differently. But this was going against thousands of years of socialisation where the expectations and responsibilities placed on both genders were fundamentally different. Gender expectation is ingrained in our psyches and despite all our efforts to treat each child as a blank slate it is impossible not to react differently albeit at an unconscious level when we meet with either gender. Researchers have even noted that the nature of talk that adults have with babies differs according to the child's gender.

Perhaps the most significant biological factor impacting on the effects of birth order are the developmental differences between boys and girls. Girls mature earlier than boys, which places them at a distinct advantage in the competitive world of the family jungle. A first-born boy whose sister comes into the world 18 months later may find that it is not long before she is as capable as he in the highly-valued areas of language development and eventually writing and reading. As eldest children frequently want to be first or the best, or at least excel compared to a sibling in the areas that parents value highly, then they will often give up or look for other ways to impress if a sibling is just as capable. After all, you can't have the glory and share it too. The maturity gap is obviously not an issue if a brother follows an eldest boy. Unless the eldest is physically smaller or perhaps has a more passive temperament he will generally be able to maintain his place on top of the sibling tree, which is where he wants to be. So the gender of a child and of those around him or her adds a fascinating dimension to the notion of birth order.

In this chapter I will look at some of the possible gender scenarios and examine how they impact on a child's birth-order personality. As human beings are fundamentally as complex as the families in which they are raised it is impossible to provide an exact picture for children in the different family scenarios. But it is possible to sketch some of the birth-order personality possibilities. I have found that if a person doesn't conform to the general characteristics of their position there is usually a logical explanation. For instance, one fellow approached me after a seminar and claimed that although he was the first-born in his family he was actually very rebellious as a child and had few of the first-born character traits that I had described. He told me his younger brother was more like a first-born. The fellow was the eldest of four children and the child who took on the first-born characteristics was the third in the family. This was quite strange, as I would have expected the second-born to be the responsible sibling. A little delving showed that both his parents were highly critical and his father, in particular, was distant and administered harsh discipline. This fellow could never please his father. Circumstances were so difficult at home that the second boy moved out at the age of four to be brought up by relatives leaving the third-born to be next in line. The third-born was favoured by his father and treated like a first-born – he was given significant responsibility that was deemed too difficult for the rather dim-witted eldest. The first-born grew to hate his father and resent his younger brother who grew into the position of the eldest, even caring for an alcoholic mother. Birth order usually makes sense once you delve a little and consider all the variables.

Oldest brother – of brothers

This boy is the boss. The oldest boy in a family throughout history has been singled out for special treatment. In the past he was the child who would not only carry the family name but also more than likely run the family farm or take over the family trade or business. This boy was special. He needed to be looked after and also trained for his future role as leader and keeper of the family flame. While most of the notions of primogeniture are confined to history there is still a strong expectation on first-born boys. One recent Australian study found that 65 per cent of parents wanted their next child to be a boy, despite the fact that current thinking indicates that boys seem to require so much attention. Boys are still the preferred option and I suspect rule the roost in most modern homes.

First-born boys often grow up quickly, become protective of their siblings and often behave in ways that please adults. They usually have a strong relationship with their mothers and can need a great deal of reassurance when their first brother is born. If his father is present and nurturing then he will in all likelihood identify strongly with him. He will help maintain order in the family seeing himself as a second father. During adolescence this relationship can become a little rocky as the eldest may compete with his father for supremacy. Life can become like a test of wills for a while as the two rams go head to head. The eldest boy will win in the end when he defeats his father in something that he values.

First-born boys often take up leadership positions and are generally successful at whatever they attempt. Their ability to focus on a goal and propensity to organise others mean that they often achieve at whatever they put their minds to. The first of two boys can be extremely harsh on his sibling – taking delight in pointing out his weaknesses and errors, while trying to keep him in his place. The rivalry between the two can be a challenge for parents, particularly for sole mothers, who may find that family life is one long argument interrupted by rare but exceptional moments of harmony where the boys seem so close that parents wonder why it isn't always the way.

Oldest brother – of sisters

The eldest boy with one sister can be a problematic position depending on the age gap and the temperament and abilities of his sister. If his sister is close in age she could be just as capable as he is and pose a threat to his supremacy. If this is the case he may start acting in a masculine way and belittle or tease his sister. As with most boys he may mistake assertion with aggression and he may spend much of his time and energy making life difficult for his sister. On the other hand, he will probably be quite protective of her and jump to her defence if she is under threat in the schoolyard or elsewhere. The opportunity to protect and even teach her some skills merely reinforces his position of superiority.

If there are two or more girls in the family then a first-born boy often becomes more easygoing, relaxed and good-natured. His competitiveness and masculinity is often softened in the company of females, and he may grow up more at ease with himself and around others. He may be less ambitious than other first-borns and gain a better balance between work and relationships as an adult. Women may be important to him in later life and he will probably be at ease with females as he has learned how to relate to them as a boy. He may relate well to them as partners and enjoy their company socially and at work.

Oldest brother – of sisters and brothers

This boy loves to play parent. Being in the position to be both boss to a sibling immediately below and possibly a nurturer to younger siblings he will probably make a great parent and an effective mentor at work. Boys in this position are often less fastidious and less obsessed with being a perfectionist than other eldest children as they generally spend some time caring for younger siblings as children so they are less obsessed with themselves.

Single boy

Research indicates that parents would prefer an only boy to an only girl. Only boys generally have a strong relationship with their mothers, which can be very intense. Only boys often have a good life as children as they are usually the centre of attention of two adults and don't have to share the limelight with anyone and a sibling never displaces them so they don't experience dethronement. It is little wonder that they expect a great deal from life and can be upset when things don't go their way. This group even as adults are not life's great sharers – they tend to keep everything to themselves including their innermost thoughts and feelings. They like to be noticed and have their achievements recognised. Only males – children and adults – like to be the centre of attention but not in a frivolous way. Recognition for work well done, awards for excellence or even praise for just turning up tend to motivate only males. Life is usually fairly serious for single boys so they often need help to lighten up.

A mother can easily smother her only son so it is useful for her to have many interests outside her family so that he doesn't become the source of all her attention. Male single children often grow up to be loners, as they generally don't pursue friendships as vigorously as other children. As a rule, single males would prefer a quiet dinner for two than a huge party unless of course they were to receive an award then they would be there in a flash.

Oldest sister – of sisters

'Mother's little helper, little sister's tormenter' is typical of many eldest sisters. The competition can be quite fierce between the eldest girl and her next sister who has displaced her. It is fiercer than if a brother has come along, because a same-sex sibling is more of a threat to the position of first-born. Often first-born girls take on the mother's role and enjoy teaching and helping their younger sisters. These girls often become 'model' children, getting a great deal of approval from parents, teachers and other adults. These compliant nurturers often treat their youngest sisters as children even as adults. Many of the shepherds that I described in Chapter 3 are first-born girls with at least one sister.

Although first-born girls are often helpful as children they can also resist any attempts by others to give them some advice. 'It is my way or no way' for many of these children. They often learn many of their lessons in life the hard way. As perfectionists they are harder on themselves than their parents or siblings could ever be. These eldest of sisters are prime candidates to take the role of superwoman as adults. They are frequently the group who try to do it all – have a successful career, have perfect kids and still keep a busy, vibrant social life. Hard work and self-sacrifice are the hallmarks of this cohort.

Oldest sister – of brothers

Men become extremely important in the life of these girls. Most likely to be Daddy's girl, she will grow accustomed to either pleasing or challenging men – probably both. The more brothers she has the greater the likelihood of her to be drawn toward men as favoured workmates and colleagues in adulthood. As an adult she will seek out male company more than that of women and will probably, much to the chagrin of the feminist movement, find a partner whom she can look after and whose children she can care for.

Anecdotal evidence suggests that many girls in this position believe that their parents value boys more highly and feel some resentment about the fact that they have been displaced in some ways. Many believe that they may be first-born but they are not the first boy so their status is somewhat lower than if a girl followed them. Although like most first-borns these girls have a strong sense of responsibility – they can be more congenial and less demanding than other first-borns.

Older sister – of brothers and sisters

These girls have a more balanced view of life than other first-born girls. Less driven than those in all-girl families and less intent on pleasing men than those born into all-male families, these girls are often independent and assertive but feel comfortable in the company of men and women. Motherhood frequently holds a strong attraction as they learned first-hand about the joy that attachment can bring, because they usually were a second mother to their younger siblings, regardless of the gender.

These women often successfully balance work and career, as they are dependent on neither to gain their life's meaning so they can gain satisfaction that comes from being successful yet detached.

Single girl

If the youngest girl in a family is 'Daddy's little princess' then an only girl is surely the queen, particularly if her parents delayed childbirth and are at a stage in their life where they can devote their financial resources and all their energy to her. Only girls are frequently self-assured, self-confident and have enormous belief in themselves. As they spend a great deal of their time in the company of adults their language skills are advanced and their level of interest is often beyond their years. This doesn't stop an only girl from throwing a tantrum if she doesn't get her own way. A single girl can swing between quiet sophisticate discussing the news of the day one minute to a silent pout the next over an issue as trivial as not getting the flavour of ice-cream that she wanted.

Parents have a tendency to protect only girls more than boys so they often don't experience the same scrapes, mishaps and problems as other children. Only girls frequently feel uncomfortable with conflict – life is remarkably conflict-free when you are an only child so they need to spend time at the homes of other children to learn not only to stick up for themselves but also that they can't always get what they want, when they want.

These girls get a strong dose of their mothers and are strongly influenced by their mother's sibling position. If her mother was the youngest then she may find her frivolous and even too playful. She will feel most comfortable with a mother who is an only child or who was born first.

Youngest brother – of brothers

Youngest boys who grew up surrounded by brothers often feel that in any group they are in they are still the youngest. It is difficult for a boy to find significance if he follows a number of boys in the family. He will probably follow in the footsteps of the eldest or the brother once removed, particularly if there is little rivalry and greater acceptance.

A youngest boy is often more daring and likely to take physical and learning risks. He is less likely to be concerned about pleasing adults so he is unencumbered by high parental expectations. He also has older brothers to break in his parents and also to look after him so a youngest boy often has more opportunity to find outlets for his adventurous spirit.

This cohort is more likely to live for the moment and less likely to plan ahead than say the eldest brother. Flexibility and spontaneity are the trademarks of these boys and they also make interesting parents. As adults they find it difficult to give up the position of youngest so they can have little propensity or tolerance for infancy. Once his children have moved beyond this stage he will enjoy having some playmates, but the task of setting limits and disciplining children will not be something he will relish. He will more than likely leave this to his partner, who if he has chosen wisely according to the principles of birth order will be a first or later-born.

Youngest brother – of sisters

Question to a youngest boy of sisters: Just how many mothers do you want?
Answer: As many as I can get.

By accident this boy is in the most cherished position of all. He is the only boy (which is the preferred gender) in the easiest position in the family – he doesn't have to try very hard to stand apart or distinguish himself. He is generally content to have others take care of him and will become adept at putting others, particularly women, in his service. In rare circumstances the youngest boy will be treated like a first-born due to his gender but even so, the youngest exercises power by using charm rather than assertion, aggression or force.

As this boy has both the advantage and misfortune of having many mothers he will probably be taken care of by women all his life. He will look to his father for guidance about how he should treat his sisters, and in turn, all women. If his father treats them kindly, respectfully and assertively then he will learn to treat them the same. Youngest boys have one great ally – their mother. To a mother youngest boys can frequently do no wrong. Mothers often defend or excuse youngest sons for misbehaviour at school or poor treatment of others.

Parents of youngest boys need to give them plenty of opportunities to make decisions for themselves and insist that their sisters don't solve all their problems and don't treat them like one of their dolls in infancy. If they are pampered and spoiled they may find it difficult joining in the active, boisterous games that other boys play.

Youngest brother – of brothers and sisters

Boys in this position can sometimes feel that they just can't compare with an older brother and they can be spoilt or over-protected by elder sisters. More than likely he will be in the happy position of relating well to both boys and girls and being adept at putting both genders in his service. He will probably do well to find a functioning first-born as a partner who will enjoy looking after this good-natured, easy-going male.

Youngest sister – of sisters

'Once a youngest sister always the youngest sister' is this girl's motto. With at least one responsible, serious girl above her she will in all likelihood develop a carefree, playful view of life with a birth-order personality to match. In families of three girls the youngest and oldest often form alliances and enjoy a better relationship with each other than with the sister in the middle.

These girls are more likely to be the family 'black sheep' or choose a career or calling that is outrageous, unconventional or creative, particularly if the first-born sister is a good student and chooses a more conservative career. This girl is usually hap-piest in large groups and will often join a variety of clubs and organisations.

Youngest girls love recognition so they need plenty of praise and pats on the back to keep them on task. Being the youngest of a gender means that it is often difficult to stand out or be different so they can be rebellious, flirtatious or just plain cute to gain attention. These girls are often precocious and reach adolescence in a social sense earlier than their sisters.

As with many youngest children these girls have two sides to their personalities. They will fight for more independence so they can enjoy similar rights as their elder sisters but they will also enjoy being indulged as the baby when it suits them.

Youngest sister – of brothers

This is a favourable position for a girl. 'Cute' and 'popular' are common descriptions of any girl fortunate enough to be born into this position. She will have less pressure to succeed than her siblings and being in all likelihood the long-awaited member of her gender she will have at least two males to put in her service. She will probably have her father wrapped around her little finger and be 'Daddy's little angel' well into her teens.

Youngest girls often become tomboys as they spent their early years playing boisterous, rough and tumble games with their brothers. These early positive experiences with boys generally help them to relate with males later in life at work and at home. Often youngest sisters have many male friends and also relate well to their male children.

Youngest sister – of brothers and sisters

Just like the youngest boy of brothers and sisters this position lends itself to more balanced and flexible personality development than youngest-borns of the same gender. These girls are often more ambitious than youngest sisters of girls and more feminine than if they only had brothers.

Like all youngest children these girls are in a favoured position as the pressure to succeed is less, they are never displaced and they spend more time alone with their parents than any other sibling.

Middle children

Middle children of siblings of the same gender are in perhaps the least favourable position in the family constellation. Middle children often get short shrift as they are stuck in the middle of two people. They frequently perceive life as being unfair and they never seem to get the same brand of attention as first- and last-borns. On the flipside they tend to be more flexible, adaptable and far less intense than their elder siblings. They have more friends than their eldest siblings and they manage to escape the baby label that is so often attached to youngest children.

Middle children are the most likely candidates to buck the family trend. If the family is full of academic achievers the middle child is the one most likely to opt out and even drop out of the school system. If the family is full of sports stars the middle child is likely to think, 'This sporty life is not for me. The others can work up a sweat if they like. I am heading for the beach.' A middle child can be found in any position but with families rarely getting above four children in western countries they are most frequently the second of three children.

Middle children frequently complain that they lack a special identity within their family. It's understandable as parents frequently introduce their children saying, 'This is our eldest Phillip. Leah is the youngest. And this is Jessica.' Neither eldest nor youngest, middles will nevertheless be different. Certainly they never seem to have their parents to themselves in quite the same way as an eldest or a youngest sibling. Parents need to be quite creative about spending some one-on-one time with their middle children so that they can build a solid relationship.

Middleness, or the notion of being squeezed between siblings, appears to be at its greatest when children are the same gender. A child who is a different gender than those surrounding him or her has a special place in the family almost by default.

Parents will invariably treat that child as special. Middles of a different gender often have general characteristics that are common to first-borns, particularly perfectionism and the need to please others. Sometimes being the first of a gender can give children the same burden as first-borns but few of the perks and privileges of being first in the family pecking order. This child could also be pampered and treated like a special jewel, which is often the case with a child of a different gender. He or she may even be the centre of attention due to their gender, being looked up to by a youngest and nurtured by the first-born. A child who is surrounded by the opposite sex needs a great deal of contact with his or her same-sex parent so that he or she can maintain their gender identity.

A middle that is the same gender as the younger sibling generally shares characteristics of two birth-order positions – first and second. If the age gap between the second and youngest is close the middle may act like an eldest sister or brother, being more likely to take the initiative in games and activities and frequently being given the baby-sitting role. A middle who is closer in age to an elder sibling than the next child will take many of his birth-order cues from above. If the first-born is a responsible, serious type of personality then the middle may become 'the problem child' engaging in destructive or anti-social behaviours. The child who is chronologically between two children will share some of the characteristics of the first-born and youngest and will be the most complex child.

Life seems to be better for middle children when they come from large families. The notion of middleness becomes blurred because most children are squeezed between siblings. Also a middle will have more opportunities to function like a first-born as there is always someone around to boss, teach, coach and nurture if they wish. Most birth-order experts agree that although middles complain as children that life is unfair, they generally make the most balanced and happiest adults as they learned to be flexible and not to expect too much in their original families.

Genetic engineering and birth order

I am often asked during seminars about the effects of genetic engineering on birth order. If two or more children were cloned using the same genetic material they might look and even sound the same but the similarities would stop there. They wouldn't necessarily have the same personalities, excel in the same areas or share the same friends. Their family position would ensure that there would be sufficient differences to make sure they were individual.

In a family of two the eldest sibling would in all likelihood adopt the characteristics of a first-born. He or she would experience the parental inexperience and anxiety, and the pressure that all first-borns face. If a second-born sibling came on the scene via genetic engineering he or she would experience the same ignominy of dethronement that all first-borns face, only it would be heightened. When faced with a clone or in effect 'another me', I suspect the competition would be absolutely fierce as our first-born would go to enormous lengths to show his parents that he or she can never be replaced. The first-born would spend much time pointing out the younger sibling's incompetencies to show that this interloper will never be as capable and competent as the first-born.

Bring a third child into the picture courtesy of genetic engineering and he or she would experience the more relaxed style of parenting that most youngest children know about. The third child would be surrounded by two siblings and adults who are more capable than he or she is and so would become adept at putting those people in his or her service. The second sibling feeling squeezed between a competitive first-born and a manipulative youngest would probably become an ultra-middle child. He or she would have all the characteristics of a middle child and then some more. Born too late to get the perks of the eldest sibling and too early to benefit from the more relaxed style of parenting that the youngest generally experiences, he or she would quite literally be a victim of poor timing.

Many people fearing the brave new world heralded by 'Dolly the Sheep' have little to fear that children will be the same. Children may look the same and have the same genetic imprint but they would not act or behave in the same ways. Their family position would ensure that there would be sufficient differences to make life more than interesting.

Chapter 8

HOW BIRTH ORDER AFFECTS YOUR MARRIAGE AND YOUR PARENTING

One of the unseen benefits of having children
is that it delivers you from your own
childishness: there's no going back.

Martin Amis

We just can't escape our birth order. It influences the way we raise kids, our choice of long-term partner and the success of that relationship. When my eldest daughter was overseas on a six-month student exchange my youngest daughter became a de facto single child. With her elder brother having left school and living more independently, mealtimes, car trips and nights at home had become a single child affair. She had no problem with that, however I nearly drove her crazy urging her to spend more time with her friends and offering endless reminders that she could have friends over to stay. I could vividly remember spending time alone with my parents when I was her age and

I hated it. My perception of Sarah's situation was influenced by both my birth-order position and my childhood experiences. The trouble was I didn't check with Sarah because she loved being a single child. After spending all her 14 years competing with two elder siblings for a slice of decent parental attention she finally had her parents to herself and she loved it.

We parent as our positions suggest

When I give a parent a piece of advice or an idea about parenting their reaction will generally be in line with their birth-order personality. For instance, in a seminar I suggested to a group of parents that they take their children to school or preschool in their pyjamas if they were having trouble getting them dressed in the morning. My suggestion met with two strong reactions, which aligned with different birth-order personalities. One group said 'no way!' while the others said 'no problem!' Those who disagreed with my suggestion were predominantly first-borns or only children and those who felt comfortable with my suggestion were mainly last-borns and seconds. The first-borns disagreed on a number of grounds that are common to that group. First-born parents have strong ideas about how children should behave and also how they should be treated. Taking children to school in a state of undress is definitely not in the scheme of reference of reasonable parenting for those born in this position. Many first-born parents measure their parenting performance, which is very important to them, by their children's behaviour. Good parents don't like to publicise their shortcomings so they were less likely to take up my suggestion.

Youngest-borns and seconds don't have such fixed notions about raising kids and are more open to ideas. They are also less worried by what others will think of them so peer pressure doesn't tend to affect them as much. They also intuitively understand that a strategy employed fairly, respectfully and with warning will not harm or scar their child for life. Youngest children, in particular, understand that children are resilient; that they don't hold grudges and that they get over such things and move on.

Youngest parents will often give their children more freedom than first-born parents. They are often more relaxed about their parenting and find it easier to be playful than those in other positions. Conversely, consistency and the ability to follow through is the challenge for youngest-born parents.

Parent types

There are generally four types of parents:
1. *Parent dictator* – perfectionist, controls children, relies on rewards and punishment for compliance, sets firm limits, and often uses praise.
2. *Parent fixer* – perfectionist, protects children, uses rewards and punishment to keep kids safe, and tends to smother and spoil children.
3. *Parent jellyfish* – inconsistent, few limits and boundaries, caring and playful, fun, and allows kids to make their own decisions.
4. *Parent coach* – consistent, uses consequences to teach responsibility, shares decision making, encourages children and influences rather than controls.

In Chapter 9, I will give more information about how to be a parent coach, which is my preferred parenting model, however from my experience first-borns tend to be parent dictators or parent fixers, neither of which are necessarily ideal for children. It tends to be in their natures to want to control rather than influence children and they set high standards for them behaviourally and academically.

And youngest children are more likely to end up being parent jellyfish – all play and little responsibility. Youngest often make far more laid-back parents and are more likely to be found playing with their children than disciplining them. Consistency is the biggest challenge for these parents. It is not that they can't be consistent it's just that many can't see the point of structure, routine and sticking rigidly to limits.

What about our choice of partners?

If it is true that opposites attract then does a couple's birth position have any impact on the success or effectiveness of the relationship? The short answer is an emphatic *yes*! What is it that attracts one person to another? Is it physical? An emphatic *yes* again! Biochemists tell us that when two human beings are attracted to each other there is a whole chemical reaction that goes on. Is attraction all about pheromones and other chemicals? *Maybe!* But once we get past the initial physical attraction then a whole lot of other stuff goes on. Do we look for our mother or father in our future life partner? Yes. If your father was the strong, reliable type will you partner up with a flake? Probably not. If your father was a domineering type who tried to run your life will you find a life partner who likes to be in charge? Probably. If you are a youngest son with two elder sisters and a doting mother will you find satisfaction with a first-born partner who had younger brothers? Probably. We can't escape our past family experiences. Just as there was usually someone in your family of origin who met your social and emotional needs, you will probably look for a life partner who will enable you to continue to meet those needs in the future. How your needs were satisfied was determined by your position in your family and also by those around you.

Let's take a closer look at each of the four positions and see what type of parents they make and the birth position of their ideal partner.

Bless first-born parents!

Oldest children generally make terrific parents as they take child rearing, like most things in life, very seriously. First-born mothers generally make caring and nurturing parents, particularly if they were given the job of looking after younger siblings. Eldest fathers are frequently strict and are notorious for being hardest on their first-born sons. First-borns generally won't miss the fact that being a parent is a responsible role so they will do it to the best of their ability. First-borns' bookshelves are stacked with parenting books (bless first-borns!) and they attend parenting seminars (bless them again!) to learn all they can. They tackle the job of child rearing as they would any other project – to the best of their abilities. Their tendency toward perfectionism however can make them very critical of their children and their errors. Many first-borns are ambitious, hard-driver personality types and they expect a great deal from their children, particularly their first-borns. Their propensity for wanting their first-born to be 'a chip off the old block' means that they find it very frustrating if their son doesn't share the same drive or ambition as them. 'What is wrong with him? I just can't get it through his head that he needs to knuckle down and work harder?' is a typical refrain of some frustrated first-born fathers.

Their propensity for perfectionism is not good news for the first-born child if both parents are first-born. That child will know first hand what *pressure* is all about. First-borns have spent most of their lives living up to the expectations and standards of others and when they finally reach parenthood they are not going to miss the opportunity to exert some standards of their own on their progeny. Unlikely to do anything by halves the first-born will be the recipient of all their thoughts, energies and focus. Lucky them! I feel for children whose parents are both first-born. The children will understand what routine and organisation is about. While they won't want for attention, they may lack parental approval, as first-born parents can be hard to please. First-borns' serious approach to parenting is exacerbated if both parents are first-borns so the more laissez faire approach to child rearing that epitomises youngests makes a great foil for first-borns. Unfortunately many first-borns don't appreciate the methods or viewpoint of youngest children. In fact, many first-borns have difficulty understanding anyone else's viewpoint but another first-born. For many first-borns the mantra is definitely 'my way or no way'.

First-borns make combative partners. By nature first-borns are flaw finders and like to be in charge so when two partners are first-born the key question to ask them is: 'Who's winning this partnership?' I am not suggesting that first-borns don't have successful partnerships. This would be foolish and extremely worrisome given the likelihood of a massive increase in partnerships between first-borns as their number increases and other positions decrease proportionately. But partnerships between first-borns can be volatile as the anthem for first-borns is captured in the Frank Sinatra signature song 'I did it my way'. Not only are first-borns competitive in marriage but also it is the little inconsequential things such as leaving dirty socks on the floor and forgetting to pay bills that drive these people crazy. First-borns find that their partnerships grow strong when one or both learn to act a little more like seconds and compromise, or act like a youngest and just relax and have some fun.

There is general agreement in research and amongst the current literature in the area that the match with the best chance of success is a partnership between a first-born and a youngest. The first-born's propensity for organisation and detail is a boon for the youngest-born, who often needs someone to get their life (as well as their lounge room) in order. First-borns benefit from being around someone who can lighten them up and give their serious attitude a shake. First-born females usually score high on any scale for their nurturing qualities. They partner up well with a youngest male who usually just loves to be taken care of (read 'mothered'). Personally I can relate to this, as I am a youngest who is married to a functional first-born. It is a case of someone who loves to protect, nurture and challenge partnering someone who just loves to have someone make the decisions and generally take good care of him.

First-borns are prone to spending more time at work than any other position. Their ambition, propensity for achievement and their drive means that many first-born men, in particular, are at risk of neglecting their most personal and treasured relationships. If they encounter difficulties at home then they are more likely to devote their time and energy to work where they are more assured of success.

Give those singles some space

Most singles I meet who are parents are determined that their children have a different childhood than their own. This primarily means that they have more than one child.

Research indicates that only or single children are the people most likely not to have children themselves. Most parents I meet who were single children are determined to have more than one child themselves. They generally cite the loneliness of growing up in the hothouse of the adult world for their determination to have more than one child themselves. Interestingly, they come into parenting with little first-hand experience of children yet many have a fierce desire to give their children a carefree, fun-loving childhood. Parents who were single children don't have a reference point in their own childhood to guide them in their own child rearing. For instance, a mother who was an only child came to me for help, as her children seemed to take sides against her whenever she disciplined one. She was perplexed that her children would retreat to each other for comfort or support whenever one was disciplined. She said her two children would laugh when she disciplined one for misbehaviour or they would both be uncooperative if she reprimanded one. I assured her that this was a sign of solidarity between her children that many parents long for. It is quite normal and healthy for children to 'gang up' temporarily on an adult who has the temerity to interfere in their affairs.

Only children parents can be ultra-hard on themselves and even harder on their children. By nature singles expect a great deal from life and this includes their children. Patience is not an only child's greatest virtue so they frequently want them to be successful straight away. Success often equates to adult standards, which places pressure on children to perform. This contradicts their wish to let their kids just be kids. Some parents who are only children treat their children like mini-adults dressing them in fashion clothes and insisting that they behave in adult ways. The oft-quoted parental line to a child of 'act your age' can mean 'act your age and then some' when uttered by a parent who was an only child.

Only fathers can have difficulty relating to their children. Their involvement is often best if it can remain at the play level but tends to drop off if children become demanding or need to be disciplined. An only father will be expected to take on more of the parenting role if his partner was also an only child. Only mothers tend to tolerate mess and noise less than other mothers and need more time to be on their own. The need for space and autonomy is an issue for single children in many aspects of their lives.

Single children need partners who are willing to be understanding and undemanding of them. Perhaps a youngest child who is a little more relaxed or a second-born who is more flexible may be the most suited to this position. Singles need their space in a relationship and don't feel comfortable being crowded or smothered. They also need time to consider ideas or proposals so don't rush them to make decisions. Singles are not used to surprises so they don't take kindly to spontaneity. A romantic night out needs to be planned ahead rather than sprung upon them at a moment's notice. As they are used to being emotionally self-sufficient single children partners are less likely to confide in their partner. Sharing emotions like sharing their time, space or possessions is not something that comes naturally to singles. It is not unusual to see two only adults living together yet living two separate lives. They may have separate careers and both respect the other's right to space and autonomy.

Seconds are easy to please

Just as second-borns are the hardest personality type to pin down as they are most strongly influenced by those around them, so they are the most difficult to figure out as parents and partners. Generally seconds make very effective parents and partners. Ironically their propensity to negotiate and compromise, which is a major plus in any relationship, can be their undoing should they partner each other. Seconds value peace and stability and they can spend a lifetime avoiding confrontation if they are married to each other. The capacity of seconds and middles to be flexible makes them good partnership material for first-borns and youngest-borns. Middles who learned as children to play and get on with siblings in the positions above and below them would carry these skills into their adult life. For instance, he or she may have learned how to compliantly follow the lead of the first-born and to ignore some of their perfectionist ways. Alternatively, they may take a strong responsible leadership role if they are partnered with a youngest. Perhaps the greatest asset that people in this cohort have and what makes them so effective in relationships is that for many of them they have lower expectations than any other birth position. Life has not always been fair to seconds so they are more resilient and more willing to settle for less.

A second-born can be more like a first or a youngest depending on circumstances such as gender, the number of siblings and the space between siblings. A second of two children can share similar characteristics with first-borns or with last-borns depending on their gender and how they were parented. A second who is a different gender may be more like a first-born and a second who is the same gender as the elder sibling may be like a youngest. Seconds though tend to accept the responsibilities of parenthood more readily than youngest-borns and are less anxious and they take a more relaxed approach to children than first-borns.

Won't those youngests ever grow up!

Youngest-borns like to have fun. They also like to be taken seriously, but not when they are raising children. Youngest-borns generally are more relaxed about their parenting and are less likely to be a fixer parent. 'Go with the flow' is more likely to be their parenting motto. Anecdotal evidence suggests that many youngest-born parents are less likely to overprotect or smother their children than first-borns.

Youngest-born parents in all likelihood were the recipients of a more relaxed style of parenting and were given greater freedom than their elder siblings. We tend to look back at our own experiences of being parented as a guide to our own interactions with children. If we were given a great deal of latitude and it did us no harm then we tend to treat our children the same way.

As the youngest of four children I was given infinitely more freedom and latitude than even the next sibling in line. Not only did I have three siblings before me to break my parents in but there was nearly a 13-year gap between the first-born and lucky me. My parents couldn't sustain the intensity over that time – and as I've mentioned they were worn out by the time I came along. They were also still busy learning how to be parents to their first-born who took a partner and had children just as I was moving through childhood. They had done the childhood thing before – they were now doing the grandparent thing. I am not saying they took their eye off the parenting ball with me but they granted me huge amounts of emotional and physical freedom, which from my perspective was beneficial. This experience impacts on the way I raise my children. While I have had a typical male's propensity to be hard on my first-born son this is nowhere near as intense as it would have been if I had been born first. After observing the expectations of first-born colleagues of their first-born sons my expectations are tame by comparison. I find it easy to stay back and allow my children to make decisions for themselves and also to learn first-hand some of life's lessons. My private logic suggests that as I was raised the same way and it did me no harm therefore it is a suitable way for me to raise my children. This view doesn't always sit well with my functioning first-born partner whose childhood was more closeted than mine. In many ways my partner tempers my view, which means there is a relatively healthy balance between developing independence and resourcefulness in children and keeping them safe.

When two youngest-borns marry or form a partnership you can be sure that they will have a good time together . . . for a while. I just don't know how the garbage is put out because neither is likely to take responsibility for anything. Discipline is not the strong point of youngest-borns so when there are two of them chaos can result. Someone needs to take responsibility and act like a first-born rather than continually passing the buck, which can be a last-born's trait. The impetuous nature of many last-borns can be a bonus if matched with a stodgy, conservative first-born type. But two impetuous last-borns can mean that projects and ideas are begun but never followed through.

Conventional wisdom suggests that youngest children make effective matches with first-borns and only children. My experience of parents and families supports this view. Their relaxed attitude is a good foil to the more pressured view of the first-born and they are more likely to sit back and enjoy being nurtured, cared for and supported by a level-headed first-born. The impetuosity of youngest-borns similarly is checked by the conservatism and caution of the first-born. There are less household projects left half-done and less grandiose plans that are not acted on when a youngest is matched with a first-born. The flipside of marrying a first-born is that they sometimes just get so exasperated with the youngest's laissez-faire attitude and 'near enough is good enough' approach to tasks that they can be domineering and dampen their fun-loving spirit.

A parenting challenge – children who don't share your birth-order

Perhaps the hardest task for any parent is to understand children who don't share the same birth position. Many first-borns for instance are exasperated by the lack of ambition of a youngest or the propensity to rebel that many seconds have. I heard a first-born mother throw her hands in the air in despair as her second-born daughter dressed like a gothic, 'Why would she dress like a slob when she has a perfectly good wardrobe to choose from?

She can have any clothes she wants yet she dresses like something from a horror movie.' It didn't help that her first-born daughter dressed conservatively. It wasn't just the choice of clothing that had this mother nonplussed. Everything her daughter did was a mystery to her. Youngest-born parents who breeze their way through life sometimes don't understand why first-borns can take life so seriously and hate making mistakes. 'I have told her a thousand times I don't care if you make mistakes just have a go. Where does this perfectionism come from?' As we tend to strongly identify with children in our own birth position we can have difficulty understanding what makes other children tick. A partnership between different birth positions can help provide the balance needed in parenting and ensure that children don't receive an overdose of one particular parenting style or even the hang-ups of one birth position.

You may have read some of the above statements about each position and shaken your head in disagreement. It's useful to remember that birth order is only a guide to the way human beings behave and interact with each other. A person's position in his or her family is just one of many factors that impact on how he or she raises children and behaves within the context of a marriage or partnership. It is one of many factors that we need to consider when working with others but it is an underrated factor nevertheless. We are not locked into behaving in ways that our birth-order position suggests. First-borns don't have to have excessively high expectations or be overly cautious or protective of their children. Singles can learn to communicate with their partners on an intimate level and second-borns can be fiercely assertive if they choose. There are no hard and fast rules only indicators.

The advantage of understanding birth order is that it provides a greater insight into your own strengths and gives you greater understanding of the motivations of those people who are different to you. This increased self-knowledge and knowledge of others enables you to more effectively work with and influence your children, partners and colleagues.

Chapter 9

PARENTING STYLE, LIFESTYLE AND BIRTH ORDER

Always keep in mind that parenting is like gardening. You plant and you wait. Some seeds take a little longer than others to grow.

Dennis Waitley

An understanding of birth order reinforces the notion that parents need to have a flexible approach to raising children. They may relate well to the first-born but they become baffled by the behaviour of their second. The first-born may have gone to bed at the first mention of the word 'bedtime story' while wild horses couldn't get the next child in the family within 10 metres of the bedroom. There is no doubt one size doesn't fit all children yet parents often get stuck in a rigid, inflexible mode and will try to fit their children into their way of thinking and parenting.

We all adopt lifestyle beliefs

Alfred Adler, the father of individual psychology and birth-order theory, believed that we all have a particular view of ourselves and our relationship with the world that becomes our guiding theme. Young children operate on a trial-and-error basis and evaluate each interaction according to the results. By the age of five or six, according to Adler, the child has developed a way of relating to the world that will help him or her achieve certain goals. A first-born who gets parents' undivided attention in early years gains a picture that by rights he or she should be the centre of attention in every relationship. The first-born will view all future interactions through the lens of this picture. It matters little if the picture or perception is inaccurate; it is subjective logic that matters.

This picture or *lifestyle* becomes a guiding principle so children will respond to different situations according to this view or belief. Lifestyle beliefs are not conscious but come as a result of a child's early interactions that attempt to meet his or her need for belonging. Lifestyle beliefs are generally couched in terms of 'I only belong when . . .'

Here are some common lifestyle beliefs:
- I only belong when I am the best.
- I only belong when I am in control.
- I only belong when I can please others.
- I only belong when I am looked after by others.
- I only belong when others approve.
- I only belong when I am in charge.
- I only belong when everyone likes me.
- I only belong when I put others first.
- I only belong when I am getting heaps of attention.
- I only belong when I can achieve.
- I only belong when I can help others.

Can you pick which birth position is most likely to adopt some of the above lifestyle beliefs?

I have to be the best

Many first-borns believe that they only belong when they are the best. So they push themselves to excel in whatever they do. This is a faulty lifestyle belief as these first-borns will often put others down rather than help them to achieve or improve. Kids and adults with this lifestyle belief will often only attempt to participate in activities when they can beat others or be the best. If they can't be the best then they won't attempt the activity for fear that they may be the worst. Many first-borns who are followed by a responsible, studious sibling become the 'best at being worst' – they become the worst student, the worst-behaved child and so on. Their parents are aware of their presence for all the wrong reasons. This may sound perverse but it is perfectly sensible if you have the lifestyle belief 'I only belong when I am the best'.

I need to be in charge

Another faulty lifestyle belief that is more likely to be shared by functional first-borns is: 'I only belong when I am in charge.' As children they can be bossy and cantankerous if other children don't follow their orders. They can be viewed as self-centred. Children who develop this lifestyle become adults who just have to be the boss. 'It is my way or no way' whether they are tackling a long-term project at work or just attending a school working bee. Their participation may begin in the background but it doesn't take long until they are giving orders and taking over. These people don't make great followers and have difficulty taking orders from anyone.

I need to be in control

Another lifestyle belief shared by first-borns is 'I only belong when I am in control'. These 'control freaks' need to be in control of whatever situation they are in. They are a strange lot. They can take huge risks in some areas of their life but they will be adamant that they won't take a risk in other areas. The common denominator is the control factor. They will take risks whether physical or intellectual if they can control the variables. If they can't control the variables then you can forget it. A colleague, who has this lifestyle, has a fear of flying that borders on unhealthy, yet he will happily jump out of an aeroplane using a parachute. It sounds bizarre, but it makes perfect sense from his viewpoint. As a passenger he has no control over what happens to the plane, however as a skydiver he is pulling the strings, so to speak.

Control freaks thrive on information as it helps them make decisions. Whether it is knowing who is picking them up after school or getting the facts about a football game these people love information. They are frequently trivia buffs storing mountains of information that helps them make sense of their world. They generally make careful, considered decisions based either on facts or on previous experience. As leaders, 'control freaks' burn out quickly as they have difficulty delegating as no-one can do as well as they can and they have difficulty laughing at themselves. They also have a great deal of difficulty apologising, as control freaks are never wrong.

I need to please

A lifestyle common to only children is 'I only belong when I am liked'. Pleasers need to be liked by others and need to keep life smooth and on an even keel. These people often give in to avoid conflict and will go to great lengths to keep everyone else happy. They believe frequently they are liked for what they do rather than who they are. They are often perfectionists who worry about how they measure up in the eyes of others. There is nothing wrong with wanting to please and put others first, however it is not healthy if that is the only way you relate to people.

A faulty lifestyle belief common among seconds and also some first-borns is 'I only belong when I can please others'. Fearing rejection or being left out, children with this lifestyle prefer to go along with others, rather than challenge their ideas. They generally possess high-level social skills being extremely emotionally literate. Careful not to offend they are always looking out for the mood of others so that their comments or actions don't put anyone offside. These pleasers have low self-esteem as they only measure up when they can make others happy. They avoid confrontation and conflict. While making others happy may seem a worthy life purpose it is not a healthy lifestyle as there will always be times when we need to be assertive and look after our own wellbeing. Balanced people with healthy self-esteem know when to be assertive and protect their individual rights and when to act generously for the greater or communal good.

Many youngest children, so used to being on the receiving end of siblings' and parents' willingness to help, develop the faulty lifestyle 'I only belong when I am looked after by others'. They become expert at putting others in their service. There is nothing wrong with this per se however if it becomes a child's guiding light then it is unlikely that they will ever have initiative or develop a mature sense of responsibility.

I have to be the centre of attention

Many youngest-borns learn early that they only count when they are in the spotlight. Kevin Leman in *The New Birth Order Book* tells how as the youngest child in his family he couldn't compete with his smarter, more capable siblings on their terms so he learned early that being the family clown paid off. The early laughs he gained from his siblings reinforced his lifestyle that 'I belong when I am the centre of attention'. So most of his behaviour was aimed at achieving this goal. At school he was the class clown, practical joker and chief mischief maker. The laughter from his peers reinforced his faulty logic that 'I only belong when I am the centre of attention'. Leman claims that even as an adult and although he has a respectable job (Leman is a psychologist, author and presenter) he still hogs the limelight and just loves to get in front of an audience and be the star attraction. He has now found legitimate, more socially acceptable ways to gain attention than he did as a child.

Lifestyles like Leman's childhood one are problematic as they dictate how people interact in every circumstance. People with these lifestyle beliefs try to belong *only if* they are the best, worst, most powerful, in control, or can please others. This makes them very inflexible.

A person with healthy lifestyle beliefs belongs through their contribution to the groups they belong to. We need to communicate to children that they belong unconditionally in our families and not by being better, brighter, funnier, cuter or by acting in other self-centred or inappropriate ways.

Self-defeating lifestyles

Some lifestyle beliefs are self-defeating and can lead to a lifetime of hardship and hurt. Do you know anyone with these lifestyles?

- I only belong when I am suffering.
- I only belong when I hurt others.
- I only belong when others mistreat me.

A lifestyle that is common for some second-borns and first-borns who were given a great deal of family responsibility as children is 'I only belong when others get what they want at my expense'. This is the martyr's motto. More common in women than men, these people learned to please others at their expense when they were young so they make this their life purpose. As adults they become doormats allowing others to control, dominate, or even put them down. Martyrs are usually adept at finding losers who will use and even abuse them.

Children who are abused or experience abusive relationships often develop these lifestyles. That is why child abuse, whether physical or psychological, is so destructive and also why abuse tends to repeat itself. As adults they become doormats or martyrs, even supporting the very people who may abuse them, making excuses for their partners who treat them poorly. Victims and martyrs tend to return to or continue the same abusive relationships they may have experienced for years as the abuse reinforces their lifestyle. This may sound perverse but remember lifestyle is about private logic and is rarely objective.

A person's lifestyle remains relatively stable, as a person tends to define new life events in line with the prior view. He or she tends to choose friends and select experiences and a style of life that reinforce existing goals and beliefs. A pleaser will probably have friends who either reinforce this belief or at least fail to challenge it and is more likely to find a controller as a long-term partner. Sometimes life-changing events such as a loss of a partner or a career can cause a person to sit back and reflect on their lifestyle.

Many people do a long-overdue lifestyle adjustment when

they reach their 40s and 50s, when they reflect on their life's achievements and direction. The infamous mid-life crisis is frequently about a person challenging their basic life beliefs or lifestyle. What have I achieved? Where am I headed? Why have I ended up doing what I do and being who I am? These are fundamental lifestyle questions that many people ask. Many people free themselves from faulty lifestyles at this stage. They often change from a lifestyle such as 'I only belong when I please or boss others' to a healthy lifestyle such as 'I can do whatever I please – others can do as they wish, but I am going to do as I please'. This change in belief is generally needed if a style of life is to change.

Birth order and lifestyle

A person's lifestyle develops within the constellation of his or her birth. A person's birth order and particular shape of the family around him or her helps to shape lifestyle. As each child's social environment within a family is different each child will draw their own conclusions and form their own perceptions that are not shared by others. Each child's birth position and experience is unique so his or her position only presents possibilities not certainty when it comes to personality and lifestyle. For instance, while first-born boys have many common elements about their social environments they will experience different sibling arrangements and experience different parenting styles, which makes it hard to predict personality type. However an understanding of birth order and the principles at work will give vital clues to help you understand your child's lifestyle. First-borns often strive to assert their dominance over the younger children and may do so by being competitive or being helpful. Youngest children frequently strive to find their place by being charming or being dependent. Alternatively, some last-borns will be high achievers in an effort to outdo siblings, particularly when the siblings are low achievers. Often middle children find their place in the family as conciliators or arbiters. To assess a child's lifestyle it is necessary to take into account birth position but more importantly look at the family dynamics and the lifestyle and activities of other siblings.

Lifestyle development is inevitable. It takes the trial and error out of living but a person's lifestyle doesn't necessarily have to be faulty or self-defeating. The key to developing a healthy lifestyle is to remove the words 'only when' from the statement. When we remove the words 'only when' we adopt a more flexible, balanced approach to living.

How do children develop faulty or self-defeating lifestyles?

The parenting style and family atmosphere that children experience contribute to the development of unhealthy lifestyles. 'Parenting style' is a broad term referring to an individual style of raising children. There are three well-recognised broad styles of child rearing that impact on lifestyle development: authoritarian, permissive and democratic (authoritative).

Authoritarian parenting (boss, dictator, controller, sergeant major, dominator)

This style of parenting has the following features:
- high in rules and routines, low in consultation and choice
- high standards, low in warmth
- strong convictions, inflexible
- high in criticism, low in training.

In this style of parenting parents use the language of compliance such as:
- 'do this now.'
- 'I won't stand for that sort of talk.'
- 'kids shouldn't do those sorts of things.'

Possible results of authoritarian parenting include:
- Children become compliant and always obey and stick to the rules.
- Children become dispirited which either delays the rebelliousness of adolescence or invites greater rebelliousness or resistance.
- Children often reject parental values if they are too rigid.

The possible effects on lifestyle development include promoting self-defeating lifestyles such as:
- I only belong when I am in control.
- I only belong when I am pleasing others.
- I only belong when I am No. 1.
- I only belong when I am the best, smartest, cutest.

Permissive parenting (laissez faire, jellyfish, spineless, weak, inconsistent)

This style of parenting has the following features:
- low in rules and routines, low in consultation
- high standards, high warmth
- few convictions, flexible
- high in praise, low in training
- want to be friends with their children.

Permissive parenting uses language such as:
- 'You weren't picked in the sports team. You can stay home

from school tomorrow if you want rather than go to the sports and barrack.'
- 'Yes, you can go to bed later. This is a good program isn't it?'
- 'I don't think that you can cope with the pressure. I'll write your teacher a note so you can miss homework tonight.'

The possible results of permissive parenting include:
- Children often lack security that limits give them and so they don't develop a sense of self-control.
- Children may not respect adults or have little regard or respect for rules. They may resent those who try to place limits on them.
- Children frequently learn to manipulate others and develop a selfish attitude to life.

Possible effects on lifestyle development include promoting faulty and self-defeating lifestyles such as:
- I only belong when others care for me.
- I only belong when I am getting attention.
- I only belong when I get what I want.
- I only belong when I look good.

Authoritative parenting (democratic, loving and firm, backbone)

This style of parenting has the following features:
- high in rules but flexible in execution
- high in consultation and choice
- high in standards, high in warmth
- high in training and teaching, high in encouragement.

Parents use the language of cooperation such as:
- 'You've broken your sister's toy, mate. What can we do to fix it up?'

- 'I wish you could stay up and watch that show but you have a big day tomorrow and you need your sleep.'
- 'You are in a bit of a bind aren't you? I'll give you a hand now but let's work out how you can do it yourself next time.'

The possible results of authoritative parenting include:
- Children's self-esteem is developed through clearly defined limits and warm relationships.
- Children from this type of parent rank highest in:
  - self-esteem
  - interest in parental and family's values
  - ability to fit in at school
  - less susceptible to peer pressure.
- Teenage children develop strong relationships with parents.
- Children have a greater sense of self-discipline and self-control.

Possible effects on lifestyle development are children encouraged to adopt a healthy lifestyle of 'I belong'.

Helping children develop an 'I belong' lifestyle

It is imperative for parents to communicate to children that they belong in their family unconditionally rather than as a result of the attributes they have. When we make comments about them being bigger, brighter, better, sillier, smarter, smaller, cuter or whatever, we focus on their attributes. When we focus on these attributes children begin to think 'I belong when I show these attributes'. This may be faulty logic but a person's worldview is a subjective view. Children are good observers but lousy interpreters. A four year old may hear his mother praise his six-year-old sister for keeping a clean bedroom and conclude that he can't keep one as clean. Spoiled children may conclude that they are entitled to receive everything they want and sick children may wrongly conclude that their parents are there to serve them even when they are back on their feet. From subjective conclusions come faulty or self-defeating lifestyles. At the basis of a self-defeating lifestyle is the belief 'I am not good enough as I am'. Lack of confidence and feelings of inferiority are behind the development of all faulty lifestyles.

Promoting inferiority – parenting practices to avoid

Three parenting practices that contribute to feelings of inferiority are:
1. Conditional acceptance
2. Comparison
3. Spoiling and overprotecting.

Conditional acceptance: When we take over responsibilities for children and impress on them their inadequacies we reinforce the notion 'I am not good enough as I am'. This is a tough one for parents, as it requires us to slow down and accept children's honest efforts as acceptable even if they don't meet lofty adult standards. Unconditional acceptance means that we accept a four year old's honest effort at bed making rather than straighten up the wrinkles. It means giving children time to practise doing up their shoelaces even though we can do it in a flash. It means that we accept children's efforts at dressing themselves even though they may have their shoes on the wrong feet (a tactful reminder may be in order here). It means that we thank a ten year old for cooking the evening meal even though the roast was more than overdone. Often parents impress children with their inadequacies and let them know in millions of tiny ways that they will improve or get better with maturity. In a household where nothing is ever good enough children soon develop feelings of inferiority, which are hidden by faulty lifestyles.

Comparison: 'Why can't you keep your room tidy like your brother?' The practice of using a child in the family as a model for achievement is one sure way of discouraging children. Many children think 'I can never be as good/clever/athletic as my sibling' so they give up rather than try in those areas.

Spoiling and overprotecting: When parents rob children of opportunities to do things for themselves they deny children the opportunity to learn that they can be useful and respected members of their family, who are able to make a significant contribution to their own and their family's wellbeing. By spoiling children and giving them whatever they want parents place them at the centre of the family. True happiness and contentment comes from giving and working for others and making a contribution to their family and other groups they belong to.

Promoting self-confidence – parenting practices to develop

Three parenting practices that promote confidence are:
1. Teaching and training
2. Development of independence
3. Encouragement.

Teaching and training: Effective parents spend part of their time teaching children and helping them acquire the skills they need to become competent contributors to their family and to other groups. Teaching and training requires patience, persistence and a willingness to spend time with children in one-on-one interactions. Teaching and training of young children is best done by doing things together. The best way for a parent to teach a young child to pack away toys is to pack them away together carefully explaining where each toy is placed.

Development of independence: Maurice Balson, the author of *Becoming Better Parents* and an inspirational lecturer in the area of psychology, would often remind students, 'Never regularly do for children the things they can do for themselves.' Balson was fond of reminding us that the development of independence in children needs to start early. When children are expected to feed themselves, dress themselves, get themselves up in the morning and perform other basic functions of independent living they learn that they are valuable contributing members of their families.

Encouragement: There are three ways to encourage children –
• build on their strengths and assets
• emphasise the activity not the result
• minimise mistakes and deficiencies.

Many parents of the current generation were raised or taught using fault-finding methods. That is, parents and teachers became expert at pointing out our deficiencies in an effort to make us improve. The intentions may have been good but the logic was faulty. There are generally two reasons why children can't do anything – lack of skill and lack of confidence. Children won't gain skills unless they feel confident that they can achieve. Constant criticisms and fault-finding approaches erode confidence and inhibit learning and true development.

In all children's activities *focus on their strengths*. Focus on what they can do, rather than on what they can't do and their confidence will grow. When you give children feedback make sure you focus on positive aspects first. 'Your written vocabulary is really improving as you read more widely, now let's do a little work on this spelling of yours' is the type of approach that works effectively with children from nought to 90.

When dealing with children *emphasise the activity not the result*. First-borns, in particular, will often evaluate themselves in terms of what they can do, rather than what they are. Such children often only complete tasks and even help at home to gain parental praise as they think they belong only when others approve of their efforts. Parental approval becomes a reward motivating children to behave in ways that please parents.

When you focus your comments on the activity or the contribution rather than the results of the activity you are removing this notion of approval. When a child comes home from school with a terrific report focus on the process rather than the product of learning. Comment on the effort your child has made, the improvement or the obvious enjoyment he or she must gain from school. 'You have really improved in your schoolwork. It must be satisfying when you put in an effort like you have and you enjoy what you are doing.' You can make these same comments regardless of the results. When you focus on the process the results will generally come anyway.

This principle is particularly useful for perfectionists and ambitious kids who set very high standards for themselves. (My book *One Step Ahead* has more information about the language of encouragement that focuses on the process rather than the results of learning.) These children often don't start activities because they can't be the best or they fail to complete activities because they can't reach the high standard they set themselves.

Remember to *minimise mistakes and deficiencies*. We need to impress on children that mistakes and errors are an integral part of the learning and self-improvement process. Many children will operate on the basis of error avoidance. They look at first glance like they are achieving their full potential because they make few mistakes but on closer inspection they are not extending themselves. For instance, in the leadership programs I have conducted in schools I have found many competent children and young people avoid public speaking tasks. They are generally more than capable but they don't want to make errors or mistakes in the public forum. They avoid taking risks so they don't extend themselves in this important leadership area.

Our training of children needs to focus on achievements rather than errors. Fortunately our education system has begun to recognise the power of minimising errors and promoting learners as risk-takers.

The importance of the early years in lifestyle development

While the community focus of childhood and education is frequently on the later years it is in fact the early years of a child's development that are fundamental to later success and wellbeing. It is the first five or six years of life which are critical in impacting on an individual's view of self and his or her relationship to the world. The impact of early childhood on wellbeing later in life is still not widely recognised or given sufficient credit. As a community we still throw far more money and put more thought and effort into the education of children in later years when it is success in the early years that will have the greatest impact. The 'I only belong when' belief is formed early and will impact on children's academic performance throughout their school life, their relationships with peers and colleagues in later life and also on their choice of a life partner. The key to healthy lifestyle development is for parents to help children feel useful and valued as they are, not as they want them to be and to encourage them to think 'we' not 'me' in all their interactions. Unconditional approval of children as they are needs to be practised day after day for healthy, balanced lifestyle development.

Chapter 10

IF TWO IS A CROWD THEN THREE CAN BE CHAOS – PARENTING SMALL FAMILIES

*If parenting first-borns means preventing
discouraged perfectionists, parenting
second-borns means watching out for rivalries.*

Kevin Leman

Question: What causes sibling rivalry?
Answer: Having more than one child.

This joke always gets a laugh in my parenting presentations but there is more than a hint of truth about it. Sibling rivalry comes with the parenting territory. If you feel uncomfortable with rivalry between siblings then maybe it is best to stop at one child. After the birth of the second child you may think you are bringing a playmate home for the first-born but in his or her eyes you have brought someone into your home who is a rival for your affection and attention. This of course is not how you see the situation but then it is your child's private logic that matters. It seems that rivalry is most intense between children adjacent to each other in the family tree.

Conventional wisdom is that parents and peers have the most significant effect on a child's development. But a child's relationship with siblings is one of the most powerful relationships of his or her life. The sibling stamp stays with a person for life. Our sibling relationships are usually intense and close. Most kids spend more time in the close proximity of a sibling than a parent. That's fine if the relationship is healthy, but diabolical if the relationship is corrosive. And many sibling relationships are far from rosy. A recent US survey showed that 21 per cent of respondents were abused physically and 32 per cent were abused emotionally by a sibling. A British survey found that abused children were twice as likely to be harmed by a sibling than a parent. It is first-born boys who are most likely to abuse siblings, particularly if they are given too much responsibility or made to act like the deputy sheriff of the family.

The current trend to have small, planned families promotes competition between siblings. Thirty-seven per cent of Australian families currently have only two children; while over a quarter of families contain three kids. In a family of over four children there will generally be at least one sibling with whom you get along or can forge a close relationship. When there are only two or three children in a family the chances of finding a soul mate or having a close encounter of the positive kind with a family member diminishes.

Rivalry is generally intense when there are only two children in a family as it is hard to escape a single sibling. As one colleague told me about her relationship with her only sibling, a sister who was two years older, 'I could never get away from her. I'd have an argument with her at night, then I'd wake up the next morning and there she would be sitting at the breakfast table with a smile on her face. It is not that I didn't like my sister when I was a kid. I did like her but there were times when I simply hated her. I think I really hated the fact that she was there in my home, in my bedroom, just in my space.' Rivalry can be like that between siblings. It is the constancy, the annoyance of living in close proximity to another human being, that fuels sibling rivalry. This constancy is magnified when there are only one or two others in your immediate social environment. Some children are more prone to rivalry due to their competitive temperaments. Could you imagine being a parent of the Waugh twins as children? Life would have been one long test match as there would have been a competitive element to everything they did.

Rivalry is most intense in two-child families when children are the same gender. The rivalry is at its fiercest when siblings are boys – red-hot if the boys are close in age. If two boys are less than 18 months apart then there is often fireworks, as the first-born hasn't had time to establish his superiority. It is not uncommon in such situations for a complete role reversal to occur with the second-born taking over the leadership role from the first-born. When this happens the first-born can easily be discouraged from belonging in useful ways and will find inappropriate ways of finding a place. In extreme cases he will stop competing and give up in areas such as academic success that parents value highly. If this happens parents need to back off and release the pressure on first-borns to perform.

The arrival of the second-born boy means dethronement for the first-born so he spends a great deal of energy trying to win back the prime (and pride of) place in the family. One way to do this is to remind his sibling and more importantly his parents that he indeed is more capable in all the ways that parents value than his sibling. The second-born then is by definition a rival for parents' attention and, more significantly, in the eyes of the first-born, approval. The younger child will invariably look up and ascertain in what areas the older sibling is more capable and branch off in a different direction. This different direction can still lead to rivalry if the children live in an achievement-oriented, high praise family. A sporting star can still be a rival for approval to a first-born who excels in the classroom if it is achievement that is valued over effort, improvement and contribution. It is for these reasons that parents should use the skills of encouragement rather than the use of praise to develop confidence in children.

The rivalry between two girls in a two-child family can be intense but it shows itself differently than with boys. Often the competition between boys is out in the open. 'I am going to beat him at that game no matter what' is the attitude of many boys. There is generally little subtlety with boys' rivalry – it is open, loud and aggressive. The competition between two sisters may not always be obvious but it is usually present nevertheless and is shown through the differences. Eldest girls frequently report that their younger sister gets more attention and more privileges than they did at the same age. Older sisters often take on the role of mother's helper or the model child to gain parental approval at the expense of their younger sister. These girls frequently become teacher's helper at primary school. They work hard at becoming a mini-version of their mothers. The second girl in the family rarely is first at anything so she really has to be different to stand out. While at first she may try to be like her oldest sister she may become more rebellious like a second-born or more dependent like a youngest to bring some attention to herself. It sounds odd that a child would act in negative ways for some attention but it is better to have your parents scratching their heads and wondering under which pumpkin patch you were found, rather than receive no acclaim at all.

Fathers are important

Fathers hold a key to successful sister relationships. They need to share themselves between the two daughters spending one-on-one time with both. Although they are unaware of it, girls want their father's attention and approval so fathers need to make sure they share themselves between both daughters. While most parents are aware of the importance of spending time with children it is also essential to spend some time with each child on their own. One-on-one time is the building block of relationships and a way of building children's self-esteem and sense of self-worth.

Rivalry between a girl and a boy is often less intense than it is when both siblings are of the same gender. For a start they don't have to share the same types of toys or clothes. They also develop gender-specific interests and hobbies, which set them apart. As both parents have their own 'chip off the old block' there is the tendency for the expectations to be high for both siblings. In other words, both children can be treated like, and thus function as, first-borns with all the privileges and hang-ups that first-borns experience. Both children are burdened by the curse of perfectionism and both tend to be a little more serious and organised than they need to be. If families of two first-born parents are on the increase, as I suspect they are, then this has fascinating implications for our future society. How many bossy, intense, organised first-borns can we cope with? From my youngest-born's perspective this is mind-blowing indeed!

Following a superstar

As a speaker at conferences I have sat in the audience and watched the presenter whom I am to follow absolutely enthral the audience. At times like this I think, 'Why didn't I go first?

I would have looked a whole lot better if the audience had seen me first.' I am sure there are many second-borns who think the same. They have an elder sibling who has their parents and every-one else enthralled so that they think, 'Why didn't I come first? I would seem a whole lot better if they had had me first'. Some children are simply a hard act to follow no matter how capable or clever the second child seems. My eldest daughter falls into 'the hard act to follow' category. A popular girl, Emma is one of those children who is blessed with considerable social skills and has the knack of succeeding in most areas to which she puts her energies. Her sister, two years her junior, has the difficult task of following in her footsteps. No matter how capable Sarah may be she has a sister who seems to eclipse her in most areas.

So how do you raise a child who follows a superstar so that they can maintain their individuality and develop a strong self-esteem? For a start parents should never compare the younger child to the superstar, even in their own minds. The younger child already assesses how they measure up compared to a sibling so you don't have to do it for them. It is also important for parents to be patient and allow the second-born time to develop their own interests and personality that help to define them as different. It is usually not until adolescence that they begin to fashion an individuality and uniqueness that sets them apart. Often children of the same gender will develop similar interests in early childhood and through primary school and will not diverge until they become adolescents.

My own family found a simple solution to the 'following a superstar' dilemma – we sent our eldest girl away. Actually, Emma went on a six-month student exchange to Denmark, which gave Sarah the chance to emerge from her shadow. In many respects, this was the normal adolescent process of becom-ing an individual with her own set of ideas, dress sense, interests and the rest, but it was hurried along in the absence of her sister.

But I'm supposed to be the best

The hardest position for any child is to be a first-born over-taken or overpowered by a younger sibling. Life is usually fine if the hierarchy is kept intact; that is, the first-born who wants to be the best actually is the best. Life can become difficult for the first-born who is closely followed by a second-born who is bigger, brighter and better or who excels in those areas that are highly valued by parents. In our current Australian society those areas highly valued by parents are academic success, sporting prowess and social success. Succeed in these key areas and you have it made. Better still, beat your younger sibling in these areas and life is sweet indeed. However life gets tricky when your younger sibling overtakes you in the school stakes, starts to outshine you on the sports field and brings home more friends than you. That's not how it's meant to be!

This scenario is increasingly common in Australia particularly when a first-born boy is followed by a sister with a two year gap or less. With girls' propensity to mature a little earlier than boys, a second-born sister outperforming and outshining her older brother is fast becoming a modern phenomenon. This situation is fine if the first-born is relaxed about the matter but more often than not the second-born can be a source of discouragement for the eldest. Rather than compete with more capable younger siblings these first-borns can easily give up. You can't lose a race that you don't enter so giving up is one way of saving face. Parental attitudes are crucial so it is important to focus your attention on children's efforts rather than results. As has been mentioned before – never compare your children.

Is the second child like a youngest child?

I am often asked whether the second child in a two-child family is really the youngest and will develop characteristics typically attributed to youngest children. As with birth-order personality, the development of children in any position is influenced by variables such as parenting styles, parental expectations and the temperament and gender of other siblings. It is quite conceivable that a second-born would develop youngest characteristics if that child was a boy with an older sister and he was treated like a youngest. It is always the next sibling up in the family tree that influences children the most, so the attitude and temperament of the eldest sibling will be instrumental in determining a second's birth-order personality. Often a second-born boy with an elder sister, in effect, has two mothers who are willing to look after him. It is up to him how this arrangement works. He may rebel against this notion or he may sit back and take the track of the youngest and put the two willing mothers in his service.

Some rivalry is good for children

If you think having three children solves the sibling rivalry puzzle then think again. As most parents will be aware having an odd number of children can present challenges as it seems one child is either continually left out or two tend to combine forces against one. Even having three friends around to play can be diabolical, as it seems that one child is often left out in the cold.

A certain amount of sibling rivalry is beneficial for children. Trying to do better than a sibling is how many children, particularly boys, extend themselves. Those games of one-upmanship or the competitive games that begin in a friendly fashion but end in all-out warfare that many siblings engage in have the effect of stretching kids so that they learn and develop new skills. Sibling rivalry generally requires children to develop a thick skin, which is helpful for negotiating difficulties at school and within the community. The inevitable squabbles that accompany sibling rivalry require children to stand up for themselves in the rough and tumble world of the schoolyard. Children in each position tend to develop their own coping skills. First-borns often revert to power, which is their birth right (or so they think) and use assertion and aggression to stick up for themselves and get their own way. Younger or later-born children usually develop a different set of skills. Many youngest children learn that charm and cuteness work far better than assertion and power when it comes to getting their own way. They also learn from an early age that persistence is a sure-fire way to defeat a power-seeker. How many first-born or older children have given in to a youngest child's tantrums, whining or good old-fashioned nagging. Second-borns need a more complex set of skills to assist them to deal with more able first-borns and their manipulative younger siblings. Some children stuck between two siblings are more likely to begin sibling conflict than to resolve it, however seconds usually develop an astonishing array of coping mechanisms. Some seconds learn to compromise with their eldest siblings and many learn to keep their opinions to themselves and just get on with it. It is little wonder that seconds are often considered more resilient and mentally tougher than children in other positions.

Not all sibling rivalry or conflict is healthy and, as I have mentioned, some sibling relationships can be abusive. Children who experience bullying or continual teasing at the hands of a more powerful or influential sibling would doubtless be considered 'at risk' if the same situation occurred at school. It is difficult to gain figures in Australia about the extent of sibling bullying and abuse but I suspect that it is far more prevalent than anyone cares to admit. Sibling bullying is insidious and its effects are long-term and harmful. Living with a sibling who teases you day after day is obviously not an ideal environment for a child who is developing a sense of self based on experiences with significant others.

Not all children within a family fight, squabble or argue with each other. After a parenting seminar where the discussion focused on the intensity of sibling rivalry that many parents experienced, a mother approached me and claimed that her children didn't fight. In fact, apart from a few squabbles they actually got on famously. There was no difference between the way they treated each other and the way they treated their friends. 'What am I doing wrong? My kids don't fight,' she said. But there is little doubt that family life can become intolerable for parents when sibling rivalry dominates every interaction between children and continual bickering, fighting and teasing becomes the norm. As described in *One Step Ahead*, my own research conducted into family life revealed that 84 per cent of parents with more than one child were significantly disturbed by sibling conflict. Approximately half these parents claimed that it was the main impediment to enjoying family life.

While the sibling dance is most likely to be performed in early and middle childhood, it is in adolescence when you decide whether your relationship with a sibling is a strong one or not. The craving that young people have for independence pushes them away from their parents. In healthy families young people usually turn to their siblings for support, advice and solidarity. The strength of a sibling relationship is often greater in families where the marriage is rocky or when parents are distant or reserved. Many families report that even when adolescent siblings get along with each other there can still be intense conflict. As in most healthy relationships the line between love and hate is a fine one. When you love someone with a passion any negative feelings you have towards a person can have a similar intensity.

Parental favouritism

It seems that parental favouritism or, at least, the perception of favouritism is one of the strongest causes of unhealthy sibling rivalry. A number of recent studies reveal that although parents claim that they don't favour one sibling over another their children have a completely different view. Children claim that parents favour one child over another when it comes to discipline and also the amount of freedom that they are granted within their family.

One sister recalls the intense resentment she experienced when she felt her sibling was treated more favourably:

There are two distinct events that I remember from my childhood.

The first event was when I was eight years old and I wanted to get my ears pierced. My parents told me that I would have to wait until my 10th birthday to get them done. My 10th birthday finally came and I got my ears pierced! But my younger sister who was seven at the time decided that she wanted hers done too. Guess what? She didn't have to wait until she was ten. She was allowed to have hers done straight away. I remember feeling upset and angry that I had to wait and she didn't.

The second event was when we were both in primary school. There were two annual trips for years six and seven. The year six class went to Mt Isa, and year seven went to Canberra. When I was in year six I was offered the choice of either the Mt Isa trip or waiting until the next year for the Canberra trip. I waited and went on the Canberra trip because it was longer and had more things to see. My sister went on the Mt Isa trip in year six and then the next year went on the Canberra trip. Again I was upset that she didn't have to choose one or the other – she got to do both.

I sometimes feel that being the oldest sibling you seem to pave the way for those who are behind you. When your younger siblings want the same things as you do, the parents just cave in!

As an adult I can look back and think, 'Well that's the way it was'. But I will never understand why my parents let my younger sister do the things that I wasn't allowed to do. I have also promised myself that I would not do the same things to my children!

Domineering and distant parenting are harmful

Parenting style impacts on the intensity and the likelihood of sibling rivalry. Hostilities between siblings are more likely to occur when parenting styles are either dominant or distant. Domineering parenting styles engender a family atmosphere where power is the major conflict resolution tool. In effect children spend a great deal of time fighting for their own rights rather than looking out for each other. Distant parenting can also be just as harmful, particularly when a first-born son is given the job of looking after his siblings with little supervision or on-the-job training. Parents need to know what is happening within their family and have the wisdom to know when children need help and assistance to resolve conflict and when to leave well-enough alone.

Parents may not be as directly influential in a child's development as siblings however parents' ability and propensity to promote family cohesion and harmonious relationships is paramount. The first rule for healthy sibling relationships is for parents to treat each child justly, which doesn't mean equally. The use of family-strengthening activities such as family rituals and a democratic parenting style help as much in binding children together as a range of individual strategies such as self-esteem building. The ability of parents to set limits and boundaries and provide adequate supervision so that children learn to stay within the boundaries of cooperative behaviour are also factors in determining how siblings get along.

So parents may not be as influential as siblings in a child's development but parents are hugely important in shaping the environment where those sibling relationships take place. A toxic, critical environment will promote corrosive relationships while a nurturing, caring environment is more likely to promote harmonious and healthy sibling relationships. But as parenting is an art, not a science, there are no guarantees regarding the behaviour of children; however effective parenting does make a huge difference.

Classic rivalry raisers

Rate yourself on these classic rivalry raisers: 1 = never, 7 = often

1. Praise one child and criticise another. This rivalry raiser never fails to drive a wedge between siblings.

1.   2.   3.   4.   5.   6.   7.

2. Compare one child to another. A comment such as 'why don't you keep your room tidy like your sister?' will ensure that there will always be one untidy bedroom in a house.

1.   2.   3.   4.   5.   6.   7.

3. Solve each and every dispute that children have between each other. It is almost impossible to enter children's disputes without taking sides and then you will be accused of favouritism.

1.   2.   3.   4.   5.   6.   7.

4. Keep a league ladder with kids' performances. Kids know exactly how they fit in regard to achievements and developmental rates without parents keeping score.

1.   2.   3.   4.   5.   6.   7.

5. Forget that kids want to be different from each other. Sometimes we dress them the same and treat them the same way yet fundamentally children want to be different to their siblings. Birth order dictates that adjacent children will differ.

1.   2.   3.   4.   5.   6.   7.

6. Expect more from one child than another. We are often hardest on our first-borns and loosen up as we move through the family.

1.   2.   3.   4.   5.   6.   7.

7. Model competitive behaviours. If you are fiercely competitive yourself children are likely to model such behaviours and attitudes.

1.   2.   3.   4.   5.   6.   7.

How to reduce sibling rivalry

Rivalry is usually at its most intense when there are only two children in a family. There are many simple, straightforward strategies parents can use to decrease the likelihood of rivalry between two children. The following seven strategies will help parents reduce, rather than eliminate rivalry between two or more siblings.

Accept children's individual differences

Acceptance of children's differences is a basic parenting principle but one that is easily forgotten. An acceptance and real tolerance of different children's interests and abilities is crucial for reducing the likelihood of sibling rivalry. Acceptance of individual differences between children is easy to write about but hard to implement. You may love the fact that one child is strong academically but you may be lukewarm about a sibling's propensity to focus efforts and energy on sport over schoolwork. You may identify fully with the serious, studious nature of one of your children but just can't fathom why another child never seems to be able to complete a set task. The fact that parents have their own hopes and dreams for their children and also have their own notion of what constitutes acceptable behaviour means that it is difficult to be accepting of children's differences – particularly of those children whose ideas, values and behaviours are different from our own.

Acceptance of individual differences is shown when parents treat children differently. Well-known Australian minister the Reverend Tim Costello put it most eloquently when he said, 'As every wise parent knows if we are going to love children the same we must treat them differently.' The 'one size fits all' approach to raising kids can cause jealousy and resentment between siblings. The strategies that parents use to promote self-esteem and even discipline must be adapted to fit different children's temperaments and stages of development. The 'it was okay for your sister so it should be okay with you' approach is the type of inflexibility that intensifies competition between siblings.

Recognise their role in the family

I remember when I asked my children to help make their grandmother feel welcome before one of her visits my eldest two children responded in conventional ways. One child helped clean the house while another put some flowers in a vase. My youngest daughter went straight to her bedroom and started to read. Puzzled and a little annoyed that she wasn't pulling her weight I asked what she was doing. She said that she was memorising a story because Grandma loves stories. My daughter was deadly serious – she was being helpful. This little episode reminded me that children help in different ways and adopt their own roles according to what gains a positive reaction. With her grandmother my youngest daughter saw herself as the storyteller. Each child looks for his or her own way of belonging and making a contribution to their family. Children will adopt different roles in the family – one may be the peacemaker, another the entertainer and another the helper. While trying to encourage each child to make a positive contribution it is important that adults accept children's ways of being family members even if they are not contributing in the way that adults would like.

Use encouragement liberally and praise sparingly

Do you praise your children when they fulfil basic bodily functions? Do you praise your children for obeying the laws of gravity? Do you give praise for simple socialisation procedures that your children practise every day?

'No', you say. Have you ever praised your children for finishing all of their meals, for staying on their bike or perhaps staying vertical on roller-blades? Or praised a toddler for their terrific smile and fantastic manners?

In the last few decades parents in many parts of the world – including the US, Britain and Australia – have enthusiastically followed the positive parenting teachings. For some parents, praise for a job well done has become like a nervous tic.

- 'You finished your meal. What a guy!'
- 'That's the best work I've ever seen!'

- 'You are such a clever little swimming girl.'
- 'You used the toilet. Let's ring grandma and tell her what a clever girl your are!'

Sound familiar? Yes most parents are well aware of the notion of praise but are we going too far?

Children gain their self-esteem from the messages that they receive and through their interactions with the world. The main developmental tasks for children under 10 are to work out what they can do and how they fit into the world. 'Am I a chump or champ?' is a question that concerns many children. Praise has been promoted as the predominant parental tool to boost children's self-esteem. But like any tool it can be misused and indeed overused so that it becomes ineffective.

I have my concerns about praise as a successful parenting strategy. Yes, it can be overused, however I have never met an adult who says that they can't cope because they were overpraised as a child. But too much praise can be discouraging. If children are told everything they do is fantastic then how will they ever really know when they have done something that really *is* fantastic? Sometimes mediocrity needs to be recognised for what it is – mediocre – rather than boosted to another level.

Encouragement is a far more powerful esteem-building tool than praise and it doesn't have the adverse side effects such as promoting sibling rivalry. The differences are slim but important. Encouragement focuses on the process of what a child does whereas praise focuses on the end result.

Encouraging comments focus on effort, improvement, involvement, enjoyment, contribution or confidence, whereas praise concerns itself with good results. An encouraging parent gives children feedback about their performance but they ensure the feedback is realistic and they work from positives rather than negatives.

An encouraging parent will note a child's efforts in toilet training and recognise that mistakes are part of the learning process so they are not too fussed about the results. Praise however is saved for a clean nappy and a full potty. Encouragement recognises that a child is participating and enjoying a game while praise focuses on winning or a fine performance. Okay, the differences are academic and it may seem like splitting hairs but the results on the potty, in a game or even at the kitchen table should concern children more than they do adults. As soon as we become more concerned about results than children we move out of areas of our concern. In short, praise is about control and encouragement is about influence.

The use of encouragement, like praise, requires some moderation and restraint for it to be effective. Just as children who gorge themselves on lollies will soon lose interest in something that was once a treat, children who are praised for every little deed will eventually need a veritable phrase book of positives to get them motivated.

Put them in the same boat when they misbehave

Are you willing to allow all the children in your family to experience the consequences of a child's misbehaviour? If two children begin fighting in front of the television are you willing to turn it off until they have resolved their problem or at least decided to act more reasonably? Are you willing to return home from an outing if one child is acting abominably so all children will miss an activity or outing? Are you willing to keep a meal on the oven warmer until the table is laid even though one child has been given that job? Many parents spend time hunting for the individual culprit when children misbehave, neglect their jobs or create a disturbance when they would be better off putting them both or all in the same boat when any child is less than perfect. Making all children responsible for each other's behaviour actually increases teamwork and stops setting children up against each other. Next time a child is too noisy in the car resist the temptation to seek out the culprit. Instead remind your children that everyone will miss the outing if the car trip continues to be noisy. You will then place responsibility to resolve the problem where it lies – with them.

Focus on solutions not the fight

So common is sibling fighting that it appears to have become the first commandment of childhood: *Thou shalt fight and argue with your brothers and sisters until your parents can stand it no longer.* How do you react when children fight and argue with each other? Do you make a plea for peace, order the combatants to their bedrooms, or lay the blame on the child who caused the infraction? It is almost impossible to stay out of children's fights because they are usually noisy and invariably one child will call on mum or dad to intervene. Your reaction can intensify the conflict and the rivalry between siblings or it can reduce the underlying competition.

Look at the nature of most disputes. They generally begin as a disagreement over some minor issue such as the choice of television programs, the result of a game, or a refusal to share. I have seen my children fight over the earth-shattering issues such as who should sit in the front seat of the car. The issues children fight over may be minor but the resulting disturbance of the peace can be extremely hard for parents to deal with. They often occur when we are busy and have little time to handle them effectively.

Children's fights usually have a number of predictable phases. The first is the quiet stage when one child annoys, niggles or even criticises another. The dispute enters phase two as the noise level rises and children become agitated or belligerent. The fight is now almost in full swing so parents need to brace themselves for stage three which is the moving phase when the fight shifts from one area of the house to another accompanied by the use of insults, shouting and door slamming. It may even become physical.

The fight usually climaxes when one or both children come to you in tears, telling tales or looking for justice with that old line, 'Mum, she hit me and I didn't do anything.' It is probably time to reach for the Walkman, turn the volume up on the television, or make yourself scarce. Anything for some peace and quiet!

There are two broad approaches that parents can adopt with sibling fighting: become involved or remain neutral. Your approach will depend on the age, maturity and ability of your children to sort out their own problems, your ability to ignore noise and your beliefs about how conflict should be resolved.

Australian psychologist and parenting authority Dr Maurice Balson, in his book *Becoming Better Parents*, recommends that parents leave children to resolve their own disputes. He says, 'If parents ignored sibling fighting and left children free to settle their own disputes, the incidence of fighting would decrease.'

Balson maintains that children fight for the benefit of their parents and when we intervene to adjudicate or punish the guilty child we are doing exactly what the children want us to do. This approach makes a great deal of sense, but as most parents know, some fights are impossible to ignore particularly when they happen under your nose.

Children often need parental assistance to help them resolve their disputes amicably. Regular family meetings or discussions provide excellent forums for resolving children's differences free from name-calling and the usual verbal noise that so often accompanies their disputes. Family meetings also give children the chance to blow off some steam or clear the air in a legitimate way.

When children want you to intervene in their disagreements let them know that you are willing to help them work out a solution, but avoid taking sides. Establish what the fight is about, rather than who started it, and offer suggestions to resolve the issue.

Of course you cannot sit down and work through every issue with kids, but through meetings or discussions you can at least give them some guidelines that they may use themselves. But don't expect children to suddenly sit down and discuss every dispute with Buddha-like wisdom if they have hurled insults at each other for years. Be realistic and look for small improvements.

If you do intervene in children's disputes make sure that you get in early before a full-scale fight occurs. Be assertive, make them aware that they are arguing and inform them of its effect on you. Invite them to either stop fighting or continue the dispute elsewhere.

Following are some ideas for handling conflict between siblings at different ages.

For children under two distraction, redirection and explaining consequences are helpful strategies for dealing with sibling conflict.

- **Distract the child causing the conflict.** If an infant hits a sibling give them a hammer and pegboard saying, 'We hit the pegboard, not people.'
- **Redirect the child's attention.** If a sibling is watching TV and a child interferes with him or her you can say 'Julie is watching TV at the moment. You can do a drawing while you are waiting for her.'

- **Explain the consequences.** Sometimes young children learn from experience but adults need to explain or make a connection. You can say 'The reason Peter hurt you was that you made him angry by taking his cars.'

Children from two to five are beginning to understand their part in the conflict. To help them:

- Check that the environment doesn't contribute to conflict – Is it cluttered? Are there enough toys?
- Explain to your child his or her place in the fight, problem or dispute. 'When you annoy your sister like that she will eventually hit you to get her message through.'
- Give some ideas about how to handle the problem. Ignore, move away, or ask them to stop.
- Highlight appropriate problem-solving behaviours. 'That was great to see you share your toy with Alex'.

For school-aged children a key approach is to encourage them to stop and think: 'How can I solve this problem myself?'

- ask the other child what he or she wants
- ignore or move away to a safe space
- give them words to use: 'Can you please stop . . .'
- use an 'I' message: 'I don't like it when you . . .'
- come to an adult for help but think: 'What do you want the adult to do?'.

Introduce family meetings at age five

The use of regular family meetings is one way to promote cohesiveness between children and reduce unnecessary conflict. They provide children with a forum to air their gripes in a controlled, safe atmosphere and also give children a chance to impact on family decision-making. I firmly believe that the regular use of family meetings is the most effective strategy parents can use to reduce rivalry between siblings and ensure harmonious sibling relationships. Family meetings work best when they are short, held on a weekly or fortnightly basis and end with a pleasant activity. Like any meeting they require effective leadership and they should follow an agenda.

Five things to do at a family meeting:

1. allocate chores
2. plan for family fun
3. discuss family issues and make decisions about issues that affect everyone
4. resolve conflict between siblings and individual concerns that they raise
5. finish with a treat such as ice cream, weekly pocket money.

The family that plays together stays together

Have you ever noticed that when you are having fun with children the fighting ceases or at least decreases? It is hard to laugh and fight at the same time. Make sure you spend some time together as a family involved in enjoyable activities such as playing games, reading a story together and other ways that promote either interaction or closeness between children. The use of rituals, such as family mealtimes, is also important to promote a sense of belonging in children. When children believe and feel that they belong to the same tribe they are more likely to stick together and look after each other when difficulties arise.

Chapter 11

SO WHAT DO I DO WITH BIRTH-ORDER INFORMATION?

I believe a working knowledge of birth order is one of the most effective ways of knowing your customers.

Kevin Leman

One of my favourite books, *How to Win Friends and Influence People* by Dale Carnegie, is widely recognised as the first manual written on the subject of human relations. First published in the 1936 in the US this book became an instant bestseller. Carnegie put forward a radical idea for its time. He claimed that success in business and the workplace was as much dependent on a person's ability to work with and relate to others as business acumen and technical expertise. He maintained the ability to understand and get along with people and win them over to your way of thinking was essential to business and social success. This notion is widely accepted today but it was new for its time. One of his key concepts was that to influence or persuade another human being you need to first understand him or her and see the world from their perspective. Fast-forward to the start of the 21st century and there is no shortage of books that provide information about working with and living alongside others. Shelves groan under the weight of books offering advice on Carnegie's new topic of 'human relations'. It seems people are still searching for clues to help them to work with, live with and relate to other people whether it is at home, at work or within the community.

A key to working effectively with others is understanding and appreciating the differences between people. Most of us instinctively feel comfortable working with people who are like us, who hold the same views, communicate in similar ways and wear clothes that are like ours. The propensity for people to feel comfortable and seek out others like themselves is perhaps the great human curse. It stops us from stretching ourselves and putting ourselves in new situations. It is also the breeding ground for intolerance. Lack of understanding is behind most conflict whether it is on an international scale or within a family. The ability to see the world through the eyes of another person is perhaps the ultimate people skill.

Birth-order knowledge is about understanding human behaviour and the differences between people. More significantly, knowledge of birth-order principles provides greater self-understanding – the first step in understanding others. When you understand yourself and your own motivations you are then in a far better position to understand others. Birth-order knowledge also helps you to gain a greater understanding of other people, which can be used in your personal relationships, in business and the workplace, and if working with children in schools or childcare settings. As any good salesperson will testify you cannot sell a product or service to anyone until you know their needs. You won't really know another person's needs until you can step inside their shoes for a while. Birth-order knowledge gives you a way of stepping into the other person's shoes without stepping on their toes.

When we first meet someone the nature of our initial inter- action is determined largely by the huge array of information which we take in instantaneously. Our first impressions about gender, age, style of dress and individual mannerisms count for a great deal. However socially aware people will adjust their reactions according to the type of person they perceive they are dealing with. Highly skilled people realise that the more infor- mation they have about others will increase the effectiveness of the communication, as they will move beyond their initial impressions. They move on to learning more about the person with whom they are interacting. Part of learning about people includes their birth order or more accurately birth-order per- sonality yet it is information that most people never consider. Knowing where a person comes in their family gives you some vital clues to their personality and to their private logic or view of the world. Whether you are in sales, management, or working with children birth-order knowledge provides impor- tant information that helps you relate better with others.

Applying birth-order knowledge to business and the workplace

Kevin Leman in *The New Birth Order Book* provides a fascinat- ing run-down on selling to people in different birth-order posi- tions. He claims that first-borns like a direct, no-nonsense selling approach in line with their direct, no-nonsense personalities. They like 'meat and potato' type information to help them make a decision and they don't respond so readily to the gloss and glitter of coloured brochures and other bells and whistles that can be used in the selling process. When selling to first-borns tell them what your service or product will do for them rather than focus on features or fads. Closing a sale to first-borns is also tricky. Leman says that first-borns like to be in control so it is a mistake to back them into a corner. The 'Now that you can see the benefits I shall show you where to sign' approach won't work with many first-borns. They are cautious and often like to take their time and consider their options. An attempt at a quick close can cause them to back off completely. First-borns need to think that they are doing the buying rather than that they are being sold to but that doesn't mean that you don't follow up with first-borns. You may need to be very persistent with this group, as they like to take their time when they buy.

Second- and middle-borns, according to Leman, value relationships so an alert salesperson will work at finding out about their clients' friends, family and interests. Unlike those direct first-borns, seconds like to be asked questions so don't be shy when selling to a second or middle child. These people generally like sales calls outside of the work environment so they respond well to social calls and promotional activities. Seconds don't mind being sold to so Leman suggests that anyone selling to them shouldn't be afraid to close the sale, but give them the chance to check with others first.

Last-borns like to play so Leman says selling to them should be a fun experience. They also like to take risks so they are more likely to try new trends than first-borns. Youngest-borns respond well to glossy brochures, graphs and PowerPoint presentations containing all the bells and whistles that first-borns tend to shun. Their impetuosity makes them more susceptible to signing on the dotted line without delay so Leman advises not to be afraid to move quickly to close a sale if they provide an opening.

Birth-order knowledge provides information that managers and human resources departments can use to match people to different tasks. It is no coincidence that some positions and jobs attract people from certain birth-order positions more than others. Precise, orderly professions such as law, accounting and engineering have a preponderance of first-borns way beyond the normal distribution while sales and promotions and artistic pursuits attract more than their fair share of youngest-borns. It is equally fascinating to match tasks and responsibilities within a workplace with a person's birth-order position. In my own business getting the match right between task and personality type has been a huge bonus, but there have been some costly lessons along the way. For instance, some years ago I employed a young lady for what I considered routine office tasks. I was disappointed with her lack of attention to detail and the slip-shod work she produced. Photocopying would be left in sloppy piles, files would be half completed and my step-by-step tele-phone answering procedures were ignored. After many discus-sions, reminders and coaching sessions we both decided that it would be in both our best interests to part company. It wasn't until some time later that I discovered that my sloppy, lack of attention to detail worker was a creative youngest-born. She was not suited to the routine tasks that I gave her. The person who replaced her was a first-born who relished the methodical work that she was required to do. She also liked the freedom that I gave her to create new systems in my office wherever she saw a need or gap.

What of the other positions of people in my office? Sue, my office manager, is a functional first-born who has the office running like clockwork – just what a creative, impulsive youngest-born like me needs. As she is actually the fourth in line of five children she has the people skills that are common to second-borns. She is a whiz at customer service and can negotiate a sale easily although she has a first-born's aversion to selling. My graphic designer, who is responsible for creating a range of products, is a last-born.

When I talk to other people in small business about birth-order task-matching of their employees the lights frequently go on for them as they realise that they have the wrong people or personality type for the required tasks. A colleague who runs a sales and marketing consultancy ironically was having difficulty finding the right person to market his seminars. Obviously his standards were high, however he had hired a number of people whom he found weren't up to the task of selling. A quick birth-order audit revealed that the past three people he had hired were all first-borns. He agreed that they were well organised but they were reticent about making phone calls. At my suggestion he hired a youngest-born as they often have the people skills and persistence needed for success in sales. My colleague promptly hired a last-born who turned out to be a sales whiz. Like many last-borns he had a sense of fun and he put his wicked sense of humour to good use to disarm people. He wasn't afraid of rejection so he didn't take the 'No thank yous' personally. Most importantly for any sales position the bulldog-like persistence that many youngest-borns develop meant that he followed prospects up again and again. When he got a prospect in his sights he took great pride in eventually wearing him or her down – he didn't mind how long it took to make a sale. I have seen my elder children worn down by the bulldog-like persistence of my youngest daughter who keeps at them if she really wants something, whether it is to watch a favourite television program or borrow an item of clothing, until they eventually give in just to get some peace and quiet.

Matching people with tasks according to their personality type and work preference is commonsense. I am not suggesting that a youngest-born can't be in charge of the office or a first-born can't make a top-gun salesperson, however the requirements of some occupations and roles suit different birth-order personalities. It is uncanny how early childhood can provide a person with the experience and background that stays with them for a lifetime. It can be a useful exercise for an employer or human resources manager to conduct a birth-order audit of their teams and determine if there is a match between broad occupation, specific tasks and birth-order personality. Frequently employee dissatisfaction or stress is due to the fact that a person is doing a job to which they are not matched or suited. This is an area where birth-order knowledge provides another dimension to the puzzle of human awareness. For information to help you conduct a birth-order audit visit www.birthordercentre.com.

Birth order and teams

Some years ago I chaired an executive committee of a voluntary organisation whose members always argue and disagree with each other. The group was divisive rather than cohesive, with everyone wanting to go their own way. Seemingly simple decisions would be hotly debated rather than simply agreed upon. The notion of consensus was foreign to most of the members who adopted the 'my way or no way' approach to decision-making. Frustrated with the lack of cohesion in the group I conducted a birth-order audit before one meeting. I asked everyone where he or she came in his or her family as a way of beginning a meeting. I was not surprised to find eight of the nine members of the group were either eldest children or functional first-borns. I was the only member who wasn't a first-born! With all those first-borns it was no wonder we had trouble reaching agreement – the committee was full of bosses. I began to look at this group in a new light and used a different strategy to allow members to take charge. I set up a number of smaller committees headed by the more experienced first-borns. I stepped back and let first-borns do what they do best – organise. As a leader I acted more as a youngest should – I delegated difficult tasks to others and kept the jobs I enjoyed for myself. My committee functioned in a far more cohesive manner when I gave those headstrong first-borns some free rein and some real responsibilities in keeping with their birth-order personalities.

One of the fascinating aspects of group dynamics is that if you leave a group intact for long enough people will eventually adopt different roles. If my group of first-borns had stayed together longer or worked more intensively together some people would have begun to take on roles more in line with second-borns and last-borns. Group work by its very nature demands that some members be initiators, some be creative types and some people need to be the fine detail people. That is the fascinating nature of groups.

This experience taught me that a leader or manager could learn a great deal about the people just by finding out people's birth order. It is essential to remember that it is not so much a person's birth position but how they function that is critical. So you not only need to find out their position but some information about others in their family. As we have already discussed a person may be born second but due to family or other circumstances may have been treated like a first-born and so that is how they function. After a birth-order seminar a participant told me how my presentation suddenly made it clear to him why he had been a low risk-taker all his life. He had never seen himself as a first-born as he was born second. He always referred to himself as a second-born however his eldest brother was born with a severe disability so his mother treated him like a first-born. He was given responsibility for looking after his elder brother and it was he who in effect broke his parents in for the subsequent siblings.

People often tell me that they don't act in ways that their position suggests. I usually ask them how they felt others treated them as children. 'Do you feel that you were treated more like a first-born, a second or middle, or a youngest child?' Remember it is the sibling above you who has the most influence but it is also necessary to consider your relationship to the sibling below. When people respond to this question they generally uncover their true birth-order position. 'Well I was treated like the second-born. There was nothing really special about me.' 'Even though I was the fourth in the family I had to look after my little brother a lot. I was treated like a first-born.'

Recently, I worked as part of a leadership team of three within an organisation that functioned like the proverbial well-oiled machine. There are many elements that contribute to the effectiveness of any team of people working toward a common cause and our group was no exception. However I believe an essential element for our success was that we had complementary birth-order personalities. There was also a good match between the roles we took on and each member's birth-order personality. The group leader was a second-born who possessed the people skills and personality typical of this position. He was a charismatic leader and a brilliant networker who used his considerable people skills to build up our membership. Like many seconds he had a propensity to handle conflict in such a way that people never felt aggrieved or that they were in the wrong. The second member of the team was a high energy first-born who took care of most of the organisational matters. She also doubled as the shepherd as she was the member who took the job of nurturing new talent and the younger members of our organisation. As the third member of the team I acted very much like a youngest-born. I became the ideas person suggesting new projects and injecting life and zest into the organisation, which suits me down to the ground. Being the youngest I am never short of an idea but I need a first-born to see the project through to completion. I was also aware that there was a first-born member who would take care of most of the fine details and see projects through to their completion.

Putting birth-order knowledge to use in schools

Few schools and teachers consider the impact of birth order on their children's learning and behaviour and very few collect data on children's birth order. Knowing children's birth-order position provides vital clues to understanding their personality, behaviour and even learning preferences.

A teacher with a class full of first-born boys will probably be in for interesting times. First-born boys can be aggressively bossy and low risk-takers. If a class has many first-born girls then there are many potential leaders of the caring, sharing variety. Regardless of the gender a teacher may find that she will have many cautious learners who need a great deal of prompting to step out of their comfort zones.

As I have mentioned earlier the curse of first-borns is that they are often perfectionists. They often procrastinate and avoid areas or activities where they can't excel. They need to be reminded constantly that excellence is different to perfection. Teachers may need to ease the pressure to perform on first-borns. The expectations they have of themselves are high enough without well-meaning adults adding to their burdens. First-borns respond well to encouragement rather than praise as the former focuses on the process of learning rather than the results. Teachers need to focus on effort, improvement and con-tributions rather than results if they are going to promote confidence in first-borns. When I was teaching I found that many first-borns strongly resisted the notion of writing a number of drafts for their stories. It wasn't the work that they objected to – they just didn't feel comfortable making mistakes on their first drafts. Just relax and write was anathema to these students whereas seconds and youngest-borns tended to lap up the freedom to make errors first and fix them later. First-borns usually like structure, which helps them feel in control. So a classroom high in routines and low in surprises may be just what first-borns want.

Statistically, close to one in five of a class will be only children so teachers had better be prepared for some confident children who may not be life's natural sharers. Single children are like first-borns in that they are fairly conservative, determined to get what they want and they hate to be wrong. These children also expect a great deal from life and are upset when things don't go their way. I also suspect that some single children are at risk of being bullied, as they haven't had much experience of sticking up for themselves in the family jungle.

If a class is filled with last-borns then a teacher had better prepare the painting easels because youngest children are often creative, free-spirited individuals. Don't ask last-borns to set up the easels though, as they are used to leaving the jobs to more capable people within their families. Life is a beach for many last-borns. Also, last-borns are more likely to challenge teachers, although not for the sake of power. They don't mind looking for different or better ways of doing things.

If a class is stacked with seconds and middle children then it is anyone's guess what it will be like. Middle children (who are most likely to be second in their family) are usually influenced by the sibling above them, so if a second-born's elder sibling was an academic star then a teacher may well have a sporty or artistic type on his or her hands. 'Middles' present most frequently with behaviour problems when children but they usually become the well-adjusted adults who are least likely to spend time having their life sorted out on a psychologist's couch.

Youngest-borns are often babied, spoiled, affectionate, outgoing and uncomplicated. The pressure is off the last-borns in terms of having to meet their parents' high expectations so they are more likely to achieve in their own ways. Creative, artistic pursuits are full of later or last-borns, whereas first-borns are more likely to end up in positions of leadership.

Last-borns tend to be more impetuous – they act now and worry about the repercussions later. The positive view is that they are more likely to stretch themselves and try new experiences than their siblings. The negative aspect for boys is that their tendency to jump first and think later on can be downright dangerous. Youngest-born girls can often be babied and have their parents jumping through hoops to satisfy them.

Last-borns can appear a little self-centred, which is probably due to the fact that they tend to do less at home to help others. Teachers need to give youngest children plenty of opportunities to help at school so make sure you save some monitors' jobs for these children. Youngest-borns benefit significantly from multiage classrooms as they get the chance every second year to be the eldest in the group. Some youngest children go their entire childhood never experiencing what it is like to be the oldest so this form of grouping children is very beneficial for them. These children are often the poorest readers in a family. One of the legacies of parents loosening up the further they go down the family is that they often neglect to read to the youngest so teachers need to be aware that youngest children often require more of their attention in these areas.

Knowledge of a child's birth order should also include an understanding of the other children in the family. If a second-born follows in the footsteps of a high-achiever then there is every likelihood that this child won't be quite as enthusiastic about learning as the elder sibling. Generally, the middle or second will be what the first-born isn't. If the first-born is responsible the next in line may well be a pest. If the first-born is serious, as they often are, the second-borns may well be easy-going and gregarious.

It is precisely for this reason that it is folly for teachers and parents to compare children with high achieving siblings. Statements such as 'Your elder sister was a star. Why can't you be more like her?' that are often muttered out of frustration only discourage middle and younger siblings. Sibling comparison shows a lack of understanding of the effects of birth order on children's personality development. The second or middle child looks above and if he or she sees a sibling who is smarter, faster or more capable then there is every chance that he or she will choose a different path to excellence. The best way to help middle or seconds achieve and reach their full potential is to assist them to find their own areas of expertise.

Schools these days collect and record a great deal of data about their students. Academic records, health information, school attendance, attendance to time-out areas, suspensions and the like, are all fastidiously recorded and kept on file. Birth-order information is generally neglected; however I suspect that the recording of children's birth-order, particularly those children with learning difficulties, students who attend time-out, school suspensions and students who report bullying behaviour, would reveal some interesting patterns. My anecdotal evidence suggests that students in certain birth-order positions are more susceptible than others in the three key areas of learning difficulties, behaviour problems and being victims of bullying. Further research into these areas from a birth-order perspective would provide vital information to assist in the early identification of groups of children who may be at risk within the school system. Individual schools and teachers can begin by conducting a birth-order audit of all the children in their school. This information can be used in a number of ways including to help with grouping children into classrooms, identifying 'at risk' children and putting preventative behaviour-management programs in place. Schools can then begin to look at the birth order of children who have learning difficulties in different curriculum areas, as well as those children with behaviour problems. This will help with the early identification of children who may be at risk and give more information about the types of assistance strategies that they can put in place.

What does the future hold?

With families shrinking rapidly the nature of children in schools will change in the coming decades. Already nearly one in every two Australians under the age of 18 is a first-born and experts claim this will increase to in excess of 60 per cent in a decade. If birth-order theory is correct and Frank Sulloway's research is accurate, in a few years' time our schools will be filled with conservative, approval-seeking, achievement-oriented, highly anxious, intense, perfectionist first-borns. About one-third of these first-borns will be only children who have all the characteristics of first-borns but with some hang-ups and problems of their own. Less than one in six children will truly be considered a youngest and you will be battling to summon up some children with a middle child syndrome (if there is such a thing) as very few children will be surrounded by others within their family.

What does it mean for schools and the community in general when a high proportion of its population is first-born and there are very few last-borns? My guess is that the nature of schools will change as the social fabric within them alters. I have concerns that the population of schools will be more conservative by nature and less likely to challenge authority or conventional ways of thinking. I also have concerns that a high preponderance of first-borns may mean that our schools will be filled with more anxious, achievement-oriented individuals who will need their academic lessons supplemented with some stress-management classes. As the number of single children increases it will become more incumbent on schools to develop social-skills programs specifically designed to help them gain the experience of living and working alongside others for extended periods. As the number of youngest children decreases schools may become more serious places where fun is something you have during lunchtime and recess. If so, no-one will notice because everyone will be too busy getting his or her work finished.

It is not just schools that need to take notice of the changing notion of families. It is a little far-fetched to suggest that the shrinking families will mean that we will produce a nation full of lawyers, policemen, teachers and accountants but few artists and creative types. However it is interesting to note that some patterns are already emerging. For instance, Australian politics is shifting dramatically to the right at a time when the number of first-borns is increasing proportionately to the rest of the population. A recently published report on matters that concern Australians revealed very much a return to traditional conservative, family values. Australians now value home, family and friends over material wealth and consumerism more than in the previous few decades. This needs to be read within the context of the September 11 tragedy in New York and the Bali bombings however the trend towards these traditional family values had been identified well before those two events. The trend is very much in line with the views and values of first-born birth-order personalities.

The significance that shrinking families has on the nature of our communities, schools and workplaces is anyone's guess. An increase in the proportion of first-borns may mean that there will be less diversity so the notion of tolerance and understanding will be more important than ever. There may be more anxiety so people will need to learn how to relax and have fun. There may be more people with a propensity to lead but fewer people willing to follow. There may be fewer people willing to challenge existing ways of thinking so our communities may become staid and stodgy. It is important to start asking questions about the effects of the changing nature of our population mix as families continue to shrink in size. The recent population debate and the asylum seeker issue have seen some significant questions raised about the size and composition of our future population. As we consider the optimum size of the Australian community and the impact of allowing more people within our borders who are seeking asylum it may be prudent to consider what our future population may look like and how it would act if nearly 50 per cent of people were first-born and fewer than 10 per cent had more than two siblings and were born last. As I have mentioned many times birth-order provides a fascinating lens through which to look at people and its effects on the behaviour and attitudes of people is underrated.

Chapter 12
PUTTING THE PIECES TOGETHER

What a father says to his children is not heard by
the world: but it will be heard by posterity.
Jean Paul Richter

As any real estate person will tell you there are only three factors worth considering: *position, position and position.* Buying the worst house or property in the best street is considerably smarter than buying a terrific property in a less than desirable location if you are looking at recouping your money and more.

Position is also important in human development. Alfred Adler really started something when he suggested all those years ago that people's position in their family affects their personality, behaviour and the way they view the world. It may seem obvious now but back then it was a new concept. And it took a later-born to propose such a radical idea.

In writing this book I set out to encourage you, the reader, to start looking at others through the lens of birth order. I believe that birth-order knowledge provides you with a deeper level of understanding of what drives and motivates people. Whether you are a parent, partner, workmate or friend, the secret to working and living successfully with others lies in understanding the differences between people. There are more personality theories and models around today than ever that attempt this noble aim. While most are useful tools providing insights into human behaviour few can beat birth-order theory for its simplicity and practicality. Most of us have an inherent knowledge of birth-order principles as they are commonsense. I also think that birth-order principles are second nature for most people as we have all lived birth order to some degree. When I talk about birth order I always gain an instant reaction from people because they can all relate to it, because we all have experiences of family in some shape or form. The simple truth is that our experiences of family leave a lasting imprint that as Kevin Leman so eloquently says '. . . can reach across time and distance to touch you in profound and sometimes disturbing ways years after you think you've "grown beyond all that"'.

Significantly, knowledge of birth order will help you understand your own place in your family and its impact on your life. Your position in your family affects your life in many ways. It influenced your levels of achievement at school, just as it influences your children's academic success. It probably determined the job you chose and it will probably impact on your children's choice of work. It will also be a determinant of the spouse you choose. Your birth order and your partner's birth position will impact on the success of your partnership. It will also impact on the type and number of friends that you have. As first-borns suffer from heart disease at twice the rate of other birth positions, where you come in your family will impact on your health as well as impacting on your life expectancy. The effects of your birth order are far-reaching and often underestimated.

Which birth position would you rather be in? Almost without exception children tell me that their position, whatever one that may be, is the worst. First-borns moan about their strict parents or the hard run that they have compared to their siblings. Seconds and middles complain about the unfairness and the disadvantages of following in another's footsteps. Last-borns point to the fact that no-one takes them seriously or that no-one ever listens to them. Every position has its advantages and disadvantages so it is best to just get on with it, regardless of your birth order. My experience working with children and young people is that those who make the best of life are those who don't get bogged down with matters that they have no control over.

In some ways whether a birth position is favourable or not will depend on your siblings and also the birth position of your parents. There are some family constellations where the odds are stacked against a child born in a certain position. That doesn't mean that a child born into a seemingly unfavourable position won't be happy or successful. Too many factors impact on children to suggest that the position in their family will mean their fates are signed, sealed and delivered. Temperament, the family frame, parenting styles and the temperaments and interests of siblings all combine to influence a child in the form-ative years. Importantly, we are cognitive beings who can decide our own fates. At least we can choose how we think, feel and behave in any given circumstance, which are vital lessons to impart to our children. We are not at the whim of our biology, nor can we blame our mothers or our siblings for our fates.

The six important elements to remember about birth order are these:

1. It is not so much a person's position in the family that is sig-nificant; it is how he or she functions. When a person doesn't line up with the prescribed birth-order personality it

is useful to look at the variables that may have caused this divergence. It usually makes sense when you understand more about a person's family background.

2. We usually take our personality cues from the sibling above us so if you are trying to work out how you or your child fit in, look at the next oldest sibling to gain an understanding. It is important to look at the whole picture when considering birth order so the more information you can gain about a person's family background the clearer the picture will be.

3. No position is better than another however each has its disadvantages and inherent strengths. Your reaction to your child's strengths and weaknesses will be influenced by your own birth-order position. Youngest-born parents find it easier to accept the negative traits of their children than eldest-born who often want to compensate for or fix shortcomings.

4. The way parents treat children is just as significant as their birth order, gender, spacing and temperament. It is parents who shape the social and physical environment in which children live.

5. A child's birth-order personality is developed in the first five or six years of life so it is the early years that are critical in a child's development.

6. Birth order is merely a determinant of a child's future not a life sentence. No system of personality is set in stone or comprehensive enough to provide a formula for development.

As I have said many times it is fascinating to look at the similarities and differences between children in families according to the perspective of birth order. It needs to be factored in when determining a whole range of issues involving children and young people.

For parents trying to understand the differences between children and trying to come to grips with rampant sibling rivalry, remember that children are trying to find their niche in the family by being different. Accept the differences and focus on the processes not the results of their activities.

For two single parents contemplating bringing together two families consider children's ages and the birth-order positions before you blend your families. Don't let birth order stop you just consider the children's birth-order positions and the impact your union may have.

For teachers planning their curriculum programs consider the impact of birth order on the way you teach children and also how you place them in social groups.

For principals and senior staff grappling with bullying behaviours in schools take note of the birth order of both the perpetrators and those on the receiving end. With the increase in both first-borns and also single children it is not surprising that bullying is on the increase. The former is more likely to bully, particularly if they are treated like the deputy sheriff at home and the latter is most at risk of being bullied.

For employers hiring young people for part-time jobs or even their first jobs take note of where they come in their family and learn something about their relationship with their siblings. This will give you a guide to how best to manage and motivate them.

And finally . . . birth-order principles can be applied to many areas of life for both children and adults. It is fun looking at others through the lens of birth order but it is a fallible system. The position of a child in his or her family is only a predictor of personality and academic and future success, but a powerful predictor nonetheless. It is definitely a factor that parents need to consider as we look for ways to raise and teach happy, well-adjusted and confident children. It is also a factor to consider when you look for ways to relate better to adults with whom you work or live. Birth order is the most underrated and least understood influencer of human behaviour yet one of the simplest and easiest to grasp. It is also a concept that makes so much commonsense – which is something that is in short supply in an age when we try to make the simple complicated and common knowledge specialised knowledge.

REFERENCES

Adler, Alfred, *Understanding Human Nature*, Greenberg, New York, 1936.

Adler, Alfred, 'The Individual Psychology of Alfred Alder', in H L Ansbacher & R R Ansbacher (eds), New York, Harper & Row, 1956, pp 379–380.

Balson, Maurice, *Becoming Better Parents*, ACER (third edition, 1989, p 72).

Costello, Tim, *Tips from a Travelling Soul-searcher*, Allen & Unwin, 1999.

Dreikurs, Rudolf, MD, 'The Courage to be Imperfect', speech, 1962.

Grose, Michael, *One Step Ahead*, Random House, 2001.

Hawkes, Tim, *Boy Oh Boy*, Pearson Education, 2001, p 18.

Konig, Karl, *Brothers and Sisters: The Order of Birth in the Family*, Anthroscopic Press, New York, 1963.

Leman, Kevin, *The New Birth Order Book*, Fleming H Revel, 2000, pp 57, 61, 62, 135, 168, 222, 290, 192.

Prior, Sanson, Smart & Oberklaid, *Australian Temperament Project*, 1983–2000, Australian Institute of Family Studies.

Richardson, Ronald, & Richdardson, Lois, *Birth Order and You*, Self-Control Press, 2000, pp 42, 155, 94.

Sulloway, Frank, *Born to Rebel*, Scribe, 1998.